Cooking with the Wines of

# Washington

# Cooking with the Wines of
# Washington

**TROY & CHERYL-LYNN TOWNSIN**

whitecap

Edited by Elaine Jones
Proofread by Lesley Cameron
Design by Michelle Mayne
Typeset by Jesse Marchand
Food photography by Tracey Kusiewicz

Regional Washington winery maps courtesy of the Washington Wine Commission.

Printed in Canada by Friesens

## LIBRARY AND ARCHIVES CANADA CATALOGUING IN PUBLICATION

Townsin, Troy, 1975–
 Cooking with the wines of Washington / Troy Townsin, Cheryl-Lynn Townsin.

Includes index.
ISBN 978-1-55285-849-3
ISBN 1-55285-849-9

1. Cookery (Wine).  2. Wine and wine making--Washington (State).
3. Wineries--Washington (State).  I. Townsin, Cheryl-Lynn, 1979–  II. Title.

TX726.T695 2007    641.6'22    C2006-904988-2

The publisher acknowledges the financial support of the Government of Canada through
the Book Publishing Industry Development Program (BPIDP) and the Province of British
Columbia through the Book Publishing Tax Credit.

## PROP SOURCES

Tools & Techniques Ltd.
250–16th Street West
Vancouver B.C. V7V 3R5
604-925-1835
www.thestoreforcooks.com

The Gourmet Warehouse
1340 East Hastings
Vancouver B.C. V5L 1S3
604-253-3022
www.gourmetwarehouse.ca

Pottery Barn
2600 Granville Street
Vancouver B.C. V6H 3H8
604-678-9897
www.potterybarn.ca

Chintz & Co.
950 Homer Street
Vancouver B.C. V6B 2W7
604-689-2022
www.chintz.com

## IMPORTANT

Those who might be at risk of salmonella poisoning (the elderly, pregnant women, young
children and those suffering from immune deficiency) should consult their doctor with
any concerns about eating raw eggs.

## HOW CAN WE IMPROVE?

We strive for excellence and value any feedback that will help make our books better.
We'd love to hear your suggestions, and if you come across information that's out of date
we'd appreciate you letting us know so we can amend future editions of the book. And
feel free to tell us which recipes you like so we can keep the book chock-full of your
favorites. You can email us at contactus@polyglotpublishing.com.

# Contents

# Introduction

WASHINGTON STATE IS RECOGNIZED THROUGHOUT THE WORLD
as a leading producer of award-winning, high-quality wine.
From the San Juan Islands of Puget Sound through the bustling
metropolis of Seattle, across the desert plateaus east of the
majestic Cascade Mountains, past dormant volcanoes to the
sunny slopes of the Yakima Valley, over fertile hills to the Walla
Walla Valley and down to the scenic shores of Lake Chelan,
vineyards are bursting with grapes that will be made into
glorious wines.

This book pays tribute to the wineries of Washington
with a collection of 100 recipes for cooking with wine. Many
of the recipes come directly from the numerous wineries
located throughout Washington. Some of the recipes are
family secrets being published here for the first time. Others
are adaptations of old classics, and some have been created by
world-renowned chefs especially for this book. All the recipes
have been tried and tested, and we're sure you'll enjoy them.

Cooking with wine can make the difference between a
good meal and a great meal. But don't forget the golden rule:
you must never cook with a wine that you wouldn't drink. This
means you shouldn't use anything labeled "cooking wine," as
these awful concoctions are full of vinegar or salt and can ruin a
perfectly good meal.

You may be surprised to learn that cooking with wine also
has certain health benefits. Studies show not only that wine is
beneficial for the heart, but also that cooking with wine helps
reduce salt intake by increasing the flavor of food. Do your
health a favor and include a little wine in your cooking!

Don't worry too much about the alcohol content of
wine when you're cooking. When wine is heated, the alcohol
in the wine is significantly reduced. However, it would require
a lot of cooking time to completely remove the alcohol, so if
someone cannot consume any alcohol, then it's safer not to
serve him or her food cooked with wine. As you work your

way through the recipes in this book you'll discover that cooking with wine is not only easy, it's also a fun, rewarding and social experience.

We're often asked about pairing the right wine with the right food. Cooking with wine can be the answer to all your "pairing" problems. When we match wines with foods, we're trying to find flavors in the food that complement the flavors in the wine. Cooking with wine infuses the food with the flavors of the wine. If you serve the same wine with your meal, you'll have a perfect match nearly every time.

Washington is abundant in magnificent fresh produce. We wholeheartedly believe in using local ingredients when preparing your meals, and a trip to Pike Place Market in Seattle lays out all the raw delectable treasures the state has to offer right before your eyes. It's mouth-watering to see fat globe artichokes from the Skagit Valley next to bright red, juicy, vine-ripened tomatoes; huge bushels of sweet corn; earthy wild mushrooms; tender shoots of asparagus; baskets of baby red potatoes and those huge, sweet Walla Walla onions. There are orchard fruits aplenty and polished apples, juicy apricots, nectarines, peaches and pears sit beside cherries, blackberries, raspberries and strawberries.

While shopping at the market, a fat silver Puget Sound salmon may fly past your face as the fishmongers show off their skill and dexterity while entertaining shoppers. But the real stars are the live Dungeness crab, Salish Sea scallops, rock cod, halibut, Olympia oysters, locally smoked albacore tuna, bay shrimp and massive geoduck clams. The butchers are stocked with San Juan Island's lamb, organic beef, free-range chicken, and farm-raised rabbit and quail. Washington is one big larder stocked full of ingredients that chefs around the world can only fantasize about.

With so much high-quality produce, it will come as no surprise to learn that Washington wineries have also risen to

## COOKING CONVERSION CHARTS

| Imperial | Metric |
| --- | --- |
| ¼ tsp | 1 mL |
| ½ tsp | 2 mL |
| 1 tsp | 5 mL |
| 2 tsp | 10 mL |
| 1 Tbsp | 15 mL |
| 2 Tbsp | 25 mL |
| ¼ cup | 50 mL |
| ⅓ cup | 75 mL |
| ½ cup | 125 mL |
| ⅔ cup | 150 mL |
| ¾ cup | 175 mL |
| 1 cup | 250 mL |

| Imperial | | Metric |
|---|---|---|
| oz | lb | |
| ¼ oz | - | 7 gm |
| ½ oz | - | 15 gm |
| 1 oz | - | 30 gm |
| 2 oz | - | 55 gm |
| 4 oz | ¼ lb | 110 gm |
| 5 oz | - | 140 gm |
| 8 oz | ½ lb | 230 gm |
| 10 oz | - | 280 gm |
| 16 oz | 1 lb | 450 gm |
| 24 oz | 1½ lb | 680 gm |
| 32 oz | 2 lb | 900 gm |

the challenge of crafting some of the world's finest beverages. The better-known wines are the dark dense Merlots, rich complex Cabernet Sauvignons, powerful buttery Chardonnays and fruity full-bodied Rieslings—but it doesn't stop there. Winemakers are also making waves with their fleshy Syrahs and are working wonders with lesser-known varieties such as Gewürztraminer, Viognier and Semillon.

In this book we've tried to include recipes that cater to as wide a range of tastes as possible, although it's only fair to warn you that we do love garlic. If there's too much garlic in a recipe for your liking, feel free to tone it down. The same goes for any other ingredients you either don't have or don't want to use. The recipes are guides for your own culinary adventures, and it's often fun to experiment and substitute.

The most important thing to remember when you're cooking for others is that your guests are there to spend time with you. Do as much preparation as you possibly can before they arrive so you can enjoy their company. This is every bit as important as good food and good wine. Pour some wine and invite your guests into the kitchen to talk while you finish making the meal. Make cooking a time to socialize and have fun.

You have the ingredients and you have the wine. This book was created to help you put the two together. It's full of inspired dishes that often combine unusual yet wonderful flavors and textures. There are simple-to-prepare dishes that you can whip up after work using what you have in the pantry, and there are exquisite, more time-consuming recipes for special occasions.

If there is wine terminology you're unfamiliar with, don't be afraid to ask about it at the wineries or your local wine store. Wine lovers are usually thrilled when they get a chance to discuss their passion with someone who is interested.

In addition to being a cookbook, this is a guide to all of

Washington's magnificent wineries, making touring a little easier and more enjoyable. You'll find a listing, by area, of all Washington's wineries, complete with maps, beginning on page 196. So get out there and enjoy Washington's spectacular scenery, visit the wineries, grab a corkscrew and a bottle of your favorite wine, and use this book to cook yourself up an unforgettable feast.

| Fahrenheit | Celsius |
| --- | --- |
| 175 | 80 |
| 200 | 95 |
| 225 | 110 |
| 250 | 120 |
| 275 | 140 |
| 300 | 150 |
| 325 | 160 |
| 350 | 180 |
| 375 | 190 |
| 400 | 200 |
| 425 | 220 |
| 450 | 230 |

# Appetizers

Compromises are for relationships, not wine.

—Sir Robert Scott Caywood

# Chinook Winery Shrimp Semillon

*featuring* CHINOOK YAKIMA VALLEY SEMILLON

1½ lb large shrimp, in the shell or peeled (your preference)

½ cup Semillon

1 pint mild chunky red salsa (we recommend San Juan Salsa Company)

fresh cilantro to taste

crusty bread

*Wendell Mackey, father of Chinook proprietor Clay Mackey, created this recipe. Winemakers Kay Simon and Clay Mackey offer a full-flavored version of Semillon each vintage. It offers a lighter, interesting alternative for those seeking a change from Chardonnay. Look for pineapple, cream soda and citrus flavors in this beautiful, dry Semillon.*

1.  Preheat the oven to 375°F. Lay the shrimp flat on the bottom of a heatproof glass baking dish (9- × 13-inch). Pour the Semillon over the shrimp.

2.  Cover the shrimp evenly with salsa. Sprinkle with cilantro.

3.  Bake for approximately 20 minutes or until the shrimp are pink and are no longer translucent.

4.  Serve in shallow bowls, with crusty bread for dunking in the sauce. Place a bowl of chopped cilantro on the table for guests to add to their taste. Provide napkins and empty bowls for any shrimp shells. Enjoy with a glass of Chinook Semillon.

SERVES 4-6

CHINOOK WINERY
Corner of Wine Country Road and
Wittkopf  Loop, Prosser
TEL: (509) 786-2725
FAX: (509) 786-2777
www.chinookwines.com
info@chinookwines.com

WINE SHOP, TOURS AND TASTINGS
Winery is open May–Oct., Sat. and
Sun. noon–5 p.m.

GETTING THERE
From I-82 take exit 82, heading
east from Seattle. At the top of the
exit turn right, heading east. About
¼ mile down turn right again onto
Whittkopf.

WINERY HIGHLIGHTS
The lovely shaded garden is a favorite
picnic spot.

# Caponata

*featuring* RIESLING

2 medium eggplants, cut in
   ½-inch cubes

¼ cup kosher salt

2 Tbsp olive oil

½ small bunch celery with
   leaves, chopped

1 sweet onion, chopped

6 cloves garlic, slivered

1 large red bell pepper, diced

½ cup Riesling

4 tomatoes, diced

1 Tbsp chopped fresh oregano

1 Tbsp chopped fresh thyme

½ cup red wine vinegar

⅓ cup capers, drained

1 cup sliced green olives

salt and freshly ground black
   pepper to taste

crusty bread

*Executive Chef Greg Masset of the Yakima Country Club has been kind enough to share some of his trade secrets with us and this is one of them. This dish is a traditional Sicilian staple that is very popular throughout Italy. Once this recipe gets around it will be very popular in your area, too.*

1. Place the diced eggplant in a colander and sprinkle with the kosher salt. Allow to sit for 30 minutes before rinsing off the salt under cold, running water.

2. Place the olive oil in a frying pan over medium heat, add the celery and sauté for 3 minutes. Add the onion, eggplant, garlic and red pepper and cook for an additional 10 minutes, stirring often. Add the wine, tomatoes, oregano and thyme and cook for an additional 15–20 minutes, until the tomatoes are soft and most of the liquid has evaporated.

3. Stir in the vinegar, capers and olives and season with salt and pepper. Transfer the mixture to a shallow pan or dish and cover. Refrigerate for at least 6 hours. Overnight is even better as the flavors will get stronger as the caponata rests.

4. Serve cold with crusty bread. If you have some water-packed mozzarella, this is also a nice addition.

SERVES 6

# Tasty Meatballs

These meatballs are a great way to get a party started. They can also be served as a main dish over rice or egg noodles. Meatballs have been on the menu for thousands of years and the ancient Roman manuscript *Apicius* claims the best meatballs of all are made with peacock! In the ancient Roman version they also use a wine sauce to coat the peacock meatballs. We think you'll find this beef version more than satisfactory.

1 cup red wine

1 can tomato sauce (8 oz)

2 Tbsp brown sugar

1 Tbsp Dijon mustard

2 cloves garlic, crushed

1 Tbsp chopped fresh basil

1½ lb ground beef

1 cup mashed potato

4 shallots, finely chopped

1 egg

4 tsp soy sauce

salt and freshly ground black pepper to taste

1. In a saucepan over high heat combine the wine, tomato sauce, sugar, mustard, garlic and basil. Bring to a boil and then reduce the heat to a simmer. Cook for 20 minutes or until the sauce has thickened to your desired consistency. Set aside and keep warm.

2. Preheat the oven to 350°F. Place the meat, potato, shallots, egg, soy sauce, salt and pepper in a bowl and mix well. Roll the meat into balls about 1 inch in diameter. Place the meatballs in a large baking dish and bake for 20 minutes, until they're browned through and no pink remains.

3. Transfer the meatballs to a platter and cover with the sauce. Serve with toothpicks.

SERVES 8–10 AS AN APPETIZER, 4 AS A MAIN DISH

# Domaine Ste. Michelle Tempura-Battered Halibut with Dipping Sauce

*featuring* DOMAINE STE. MICHELLE FRIZZANTE

½ cup soy sauce

½ cup mirin (rice wine)

2 Tbsp water

2 Tbsp minced green onion

1 Tbsp sesame seeds

4 cups all-purpose flour

3 Tbsp cornstarch

1 Tbsp baking powder

2 tsp salt

2 tsp sugar

3 cups cold sparkling wine

3 lb halibut, cut into 1-oz pieces

canola or peanut oil for frying

*Executive Chef Janet Hedstrom has created this recipe using Frizzante, a creamy sparkling wine crafted in the traditional méthode champenoise. This blend of high-quality Washington State Chardonnay and Pinot Noir is a fruity, refreshing and easy-to-drink wine expressing notes of apple cider, pear and candied apples.*

*1.* Start by making a dipping sauce. Whisk the soy sauce, mirin, water, green onion and sesame seeds in a bowl. Set aside.

*2.* To make the batter, stir 3 cups of the flour with the cornstarch, baking powder, salt and sugar. Add the sparkling wine and whisk until just blended. Strain through a large-holed sieve into another bowl. (This batter can also be used for vegetables or chicken.)

*3.* Heat 2 inches of oil in a large, deep frying pan to 365°F. Working in batches, dredge the fish in the remaining 1 cup of flour, shaking off the excess. Dip the fish in the batter and fry until golden brown, about 3–4 minutes. Transfer to paper towels to drain. Keep warm in the oven at a low temperature while you fry the remaining fish.

*4.* Serve the halibut with the dipping sauce. Accompany this feast with a glass of Domaine Ste. Michelle Frizzante.

SERVES 10–12

**DOMAINE STE. MICHELLE**

14111 NE 145th Street, Woodinville

TEL: (425) 488-1133 or

1 (866) 701-3178

FAX: (425) 415-3657

www.domaine-ste-michelle.com

info@domaine-ste-michelle.com

WINE SHOP, TOURS AND TASTINGS
Complimentary tours and tastings
offered daily 10 a.m.–4:30 p.m.
Gift and wine shop open daily
10 a.m.–5 p.m.

GETTING THERE
From I-405 take exit 23 heading east.
Get in the right lane and take the
first exit for Highway 202. Go down
the hill and under the train trestle
to the stoplight at NE 175th Street.
Turn right and cross over the railroad
tracks to the 4-way stop. Turn left
and take Highway 202 approximately
2 miles to the winery.

WINERY HIGHLIGHTS
In 1978, when Domaine Ste. Michelle
released its first sparkling wine, a
1974 Blanc de Noirs, Washington
was an unknown region in the
world of wine. Since then, Domaine
Ste. Michelle sparkling wines have
received hundreds of medals in
domestic and international wine
competitions.

# Sparkling Wine

*"It's like drinking the stars!" exclaimed Benedictine monk Dom Perignon as he sipped on a glass of champagne. Champagne is named for the region in France where sparkling wine achieved worldwide fame. All wine that undergoes a second fermentation, carbonation, is called sparkling wine. International law forbids most other wine regions from using the term "champagne" to label sparkling wine, although in Washington many wineries use the same methods as those employed in France to make the bubbly beverage. These are usually labeled "méthode champenoise" or "fermented in this bottle."*

*Other countries have created their own regional names to distinguish their versions of this festive drink. It is called "cava" in Spain, "spumante" in Italy and "sekt" in Germany and Austria.*

*Sparkling wine should be served chilled. This can be done quickly by placing the bottle in a sink full of ice and water. When opening a bottle of sparkling wine, carefully remove the foil cage, being sure not to point the bottle at anyone. Then grip the cork firmly and gently turn the bottle, easing the cork free.*

*The aroma should be clean and fresh, and citrus notes in the wine are usually a good sign. The smaller the bubbles the better, as they create a creamy sensation as opposed to the "soda water fizz" created by large bubbles.*

*Sparkling wine is often consumed only on special occasions, but this need not be the case as it pairs well with most types of food. It's especially wonderful at breakfast and it's well worth investing in a sparkling wine sealer so you can save some of the previous night's bottle especially for this reason.*

# Latah Creek's Salmon Mousse

*featuring* LATAH CREEK JOHANNISBERG RIESLING

1 envelope unflavored gelatin
(¼ oz)

¼ cup cold Riesling

½ cup boiling water

½ cup mayonnaise

1 Tbsp lemon juice

1 Tbsp finely grated onion

dash Tabasco sauce

¼ tsp sweet paprika

1 tsp salt

2 Tbsp finely chopped fresh dill

2 cups fresh poached salmon,
finely flaked (or canned
salmon)

1 cup whipping cream

*This recipe comes from Ellena Conway of Latah Creek Wine Cellars. She is an incredible cook who has released her own cookbook, available at the winery. This recipe also works very well with crab; just replace the salmon with the same amount of freshly cooked crabmeat. The Latah Creek Rieslings consistently receive high marks in local and national wine competitions.*

*1.* In a large mixing bowl soften the gelatin in the cold wine. Stir in the boiling water and whisk slowly until the gelatin dissolves completely. Cool to room temperature.

*2.* Whisk in the mayonnaise, lemon juice, onion, Tabasco, paprika, salt and dill. Stir to blend and refrigerate for about 20 minutes or until the mixture begins to thicken slightly.

*3.* Fold in the salmon. In a separate bowl whip the cream until it's fluffy and peaks form. Fold the cream gently into the salmon mixture.

*4.* Transfer the mixture to a 6- to 8-cup mold, cover and refrigerate for at least 4 hours.

*5.* Serve on toasts, black bread or crackers. This is delicious with a chilled bottle of Latah Creek Johannisberg Riesling.

SERVES 12

**LATAH CREEK WINERY**
13030 East Indiana Avenue, Spokane
TEL: (509) 926-0164 or
1 (800) LatahCreek
www.latahcreek.com

WINE SHOP, TOURS AND TASTINGS
Open daily 9 a.m.–5 p.m.

GETTING THERE
The winery and gift shop are
conveniently located in the Spokane
Valley just off I-90 at the Pines Road
exit. From I-90 take exit 289, turning
north on Pines Road. Drive north
to Indiana, the first street with a
stoplight, and turn right. Proceed
east on Indiana about 2 blocks to
the winery.

WINERY HIGHLIGHTS
Latah Creek's award-winning wines
can be sampled at your leisure while
you tour the adjoining winemaking
facilities. Bring a picnic to enjoy in
the large courtyard.

# Chicken Wings Baked in Mustard and Wine

4 lb chicken wings

½ cup butter, melted

⅔ cup Dijon mustard

2 cloves garlic, crushed

½ cup dry white wine

salt and freshly ground black
    pepper to taste

*Chicken wings are always a winner, whether you're having a fancy dinner or a wild keg party. This simple recipe can easily be adjusted for more or fewer wings.*

1. Preheat the oven to 350°F. Disjoint the chicken wings and discard the tips. Put the chicken wings on a baking sheet.

2. Mix the melted butter, mustard, garlic, wine, salt and pepper in a small bowl. Brush the mixture over all sides of the wings. Use all the mixture.

3. Bake for about 45 minutes, until the chicken is cooked through. Check after 35 minutes and if it seems to be browning too fast on top, cover with a sheet of foil for the final 10 minutes.

SERVES 6–8

# Water Chestnuts Wrapped in Bacon

*Simple to make, yet delicious, these water chestnuts take on a lot of the flavor of the wine. Serve them on a platter; the toothpicks make for easy handling.*

¼ cup red wine

2 Tbsp brown sugar

1 can whole water chestnuts, drained (8 oz)

½ lb bacon rashers, slices cut in half

1. Mix the wine and brown sugar in a small bowl. Add the water chestnuts, ensuring they are well covered with the wine mixture. Marinate for 2 hours.

2. Preheat the oven to 350°F. Wrap each water chestnut with a strip of bacon and secure with a pre-soaked toothpick. Place on a rack in a small baking dish and bake for 30 minutes or until the bacon is crisp. Serve hot.

SERVES 6

# Preston Premium Wine-Stuffed Mushrooms

*featuring* PRESTON PREMIUM WINES CHARDONNAY

**12 mushrooms (medium-sized)**

**¼ cup butter**

**1 tsp crushed or finely chopped fresh garlic**

**½ cup Chardonnay**

**½ cup sliced green onions**

**½ cup diced celery**

**1 cup grated cheddar cheese**

*Chardonnay and mushrooms make a great match, as is proved in this mouth-watering recipe created by Cathy Preston-Mouncer. The Preston Chardonnay is aged in French oak for a short time to create a more fruit-forward wine with a hint of citrus flavor and a creamy vanilla finish.*

1. Preheat the oven to 350°F. Remove the stems from the mushrooms and discard. Hollow out the mushroom caps (a grapefruit spoon works great), saving all the cap meat. Dice it and set aside in a small bowl. Place the mushroom caps in a baking dish and set aside.

2. Melt the butter in a sauté pan over medium heat. Add the garlic and sauté for 1 minute. Add the wine, onions, mushroom meat and celery and cook for about 5 minutes, until tender.

3. Remove the pan from the heat and stir in ½ cup of the cheese. Stuff the mixture into the mushroom caps and sprinkle with the remaining cheese. Bake for 15–20 minutes and serve warm. Accompany with a glass of the Chardonnay to fully experience the incredible marriage between mushrooms and wine.

SERVES 4–8

**PRESTON PREMIUM WINES**
502 East Vineyard Drive, Pasco
TEL: (509) 545-1990
FAX: (509) 545-1098
www.prestonwines.com

WINE SHOP, TOURS AND TASTINGS
Tasting room open daily
10 a.m.–5:30 p.m.

GETTING THERE
The winery is located in southeastern
Washington in the Columbia Valley.
It is just 5 miles north of Pasco on
Highway 395.

WINERY HIGHLIGHTS
This has been a family-owned and
-operated winery since the 1970s. It
is a top spot to celebrate a wedding
or other special occasion.

# Baked Brie and Pesto Dip

*featuring* RIESLING

¼ cup **Riesling**

8 oz **brie, chopped**

8 oz **cream cheese, chopped**

2 oz **Parmesan cheese, grated**

3 Tbsp **pesto**

*This is a simple dip you can throw together to impress everyone. Baked brie is one of those foods that can make your mouth water just by thinking about it. Combine that with wine and pesto and you're onto a winner!*

1. Preheat the oven to 350°F. In a small baking dish combine all the ingredients and mix together well.

2. Bake for 20–25 minutes, until the texture is creamy and gooey.

3. Best served with crusty bread, but you could also try crackers or even tortilla chips.

SERVES 6

# Baked Crab Avocado

*featuring* SAUVIGNON BLANC

*This simple recipe only takes minutes to prepare, so you'll be dining in style in no time at all. Vary it by using fresh crab, prawns or even cooked salmon.*

2 large avocados

2 Tbsp butter

¼ cup finely chopped red onion

2 Tbsp all-purpose flour

¼ cup white wine

½ cup whole milk

1 tsp Dijon mustard

1 tsp Tabasco sauce

1 tsp lemon juice

2 cloves garlic, crushed

1 can crabmeat (6 oz)

salt and black pepper to taste

⅓ cup grated Parmesan cheese

1. Preheat the oven to 400°F. Cut the avocados in half lengthwise, cutting to the pit and twisting the halves slightly to separate from the pit. Remove the pit and place the halves cut side up on a baking tray.

2. Melt the butter in a small saucepan over medium heat. Add the onion and sauté for 2–3 minutes until soft. Stir in the flour and cook for 1–2 minutes to form a roux.

3. Slowly stir in the wine and milk. Stir in the mustard, Tabasco, lemon juice and garlic. Bring to a simmer and cook for 4 minutes.

4. Stir in the crab and simmer for an additional 2 minutes. Season with salt and pepper. Set aside to cool slightly before transferring the mixture into the hollow of the avocado halves, using all of the mixture. Cover with the Parmesan cheese.

5. Bake for about 12 minutes or until the cheese is melted, bubbly and golden brown. Yum!

SERVES 4

# Salads

## Wino Forever

*—Actor Johnny Depp's tattoo used to read "Winona Forever"
to show his love for his partner Winona Ryder. When they
split up he had it altered.*

# Gordon Brothers Cellars Mixed Greens with Chardonnay Vinaigrette

*featuring* GORDON BROTHERS CELLARS CHARDONNAY

**2 Tbsp Chardonnay**

**1 tsp minced fresh tarragon**

**1 tsp crushed garlic**

**1 tsp minced fresh chives**

**½ cup extra virgin olive oil**

**4–6 generous handfuls spring greens**

**1 small cucumber, sliced**

**2–3 cups grape tomatoes**

**salt and white pepper to taste**

*Chef Andy Craig of Castle Catering in Richland has come up with this marvelous and simple salad dressing that will delight your guests. Gordon Brothers Chardonnay is smooth and balanced, with a combination of pear, peach and vanilla flavors. Lively acids give the salad complex flavors that linger on the palate.*

1. Combine the Chardonnay and herbs in a small bowl.

2. Slowly whisk in the olive oil; be careful not to add the oil too quickly or the vinaigrette will separate.

3. Toss with the greens and garnish with grape tomatoes and cucumber slices.

SERVES 4–6

**GORDON BROTHERS CELLARS**
671 Levey Road, Pasco
TEL: (509) 547-6331
FAX: (509) 547-6305
www.gordonwines.com
info@gordonwines.com

WINE SHOP, TOURS AND TASTINGS
Open 2 weekends a year for tasting.
Although they aren't open year-
round, they will try to accommodate
appointments.

GETTING THERE
Head east on Highway 12 and take
the Kahlotus exit. Head northeast on
the Kahlotus Highway and follow for
10 miles. Turn right on Levey Road
and follow for about ¾ of a mile until
you see the second Gordon Brothers
sign on the left.

WINERY HIGHLIGHTS
Gordon Brothers Cellars, a family-
owned and -operated winery since
1980, is located in the Columbia
Valley in the heart of Washington
State. They pride themselves on
superb handcrafted wines from their
own estate-grown grapes.

# Wine Country Picnic Potato Salad

*featuring* CHARDONNAY

1 red bell pepper

4 lb fingerling potatoes
   (preferably Yakima Valley
   banana type)

2 cups Chardonnay

¾ cup olive oil

¼ cup champagne vinegar

2 cloves garlic, finely chopped

2 Tbsp finely chopped red
   onion

1 Tbsp Dijon mustard

salt and freshly ground black
   pepper to taste

*This is another great recipe that comes courtesy of Executive Chef Greg Masset at the Yakima Country Club. Washington doesn't have Idaho's reputation for growing potatoes, but it's interesting to note that the Yakima Valley produces more potatoes per acre than anywhere in the entire United States!*

*1.* Roast the red pepper by placing it under the broiler for 5–10 minutes and turning frequently. Blacken the skin all over, but do not char the flesh. Remove the blackened pepper from the broiler and put it in a plastic or paper bag. Close the bag and set aside for 5 minutes. Rub off the blackened skin and remove the core. Chop the flesh into pieces and set aside.

*2.* Put the potatoes in a pot with the wine. Top up with water until the potatoes are just covered. Bring to a boil and reduce the heat to a simmer. Cook the potatoes until they are barely tender, about 15–20 minutes. Remove from the heat, drain and refrigerate.

*3.* To make the dressing, combine the oil, vinegar, garlic, onion, mustard, salt and pepper in a large bowl. Cut the chilled potatoes into bite-sized pieces and add them to the bowl along with the red pepper.

*4.* Toss well and allow some time for the flavors to marry. However, this is just too good not to have a little taste right now!

SERVES 8

# Chardonnay

*pronounced (SHAR-DOE-NAY)*

*Chardonnay is probably still the world's hippest grape.
This is the grape that winemakers in France turn into the
famous white Burgundy wines. Many believe the artistry of
the winemaker is most apparent in Chardonnay. Its origins
can be traced back to Burgundy's Côte d'Or.*

*Chardonnay is often aged in oak barrels, which can give
the wine overtones of vanilla or buttery toast. In the 1990s,
some wineries started producing unoaked Chardonnay
and the trend has really taken off. As an experiment,
try unoaked Chardonnay and then oaked Chardonnay to
discover what effect oak has on the flavor. Chardonnay can
be aged in the bottle, although it will not last as long as
most red wines.*

*Chardonnay is the most commonly planted white grape in
all of Washington. Most of the plantings are in the east of
the state and the wine produced is generally considered to
be "crisper" than from other regions.*

*Chardonnay is almost always dry. It can contain diverse
flavors, from citrus to apples; even figs and pineapple are
not uncommon. Some wonderful pairings for Chardonnay
include fish, mussels, lobster, crab, chicken and pork.*

# Hinzerling's Pear, Port, Cheese and Walnut Salad

*featuring* HINZERLING THREE MUSES RUBY PORT

1½ cups walnuts

¼ lb fresh spinach

¾ lb mixed salad greens

2 medium-ripe pears

2 cups crumbled sharp cheese (try Tillamook Extra Sharp Aged Cheddar, Stilton, Gorgonzola or Oregon Blue)

1 cup port

1 Tbsp brown sugar

¼ cup good-quality balsamic vinegar

¾ cup extra virgin olive oil

freshly ground black pepper (optional)

*This salad, adapted by Hinzerling from a recipe by the Walnut Marketing Board, makes a great starter for any dinner. The port is made with Cabernet, Merlot and Lemberger (the three muses). This port also pairs well with cheese and/or not-too-sweet chocolate.*

1. Preheat the oven to 350°F. Spread the walnuts on a baking sheet and toast until lightly browned, about 5–10 minutes. Watch them carefully as they can burn quickly. Coarsely chop the toasted walnuts and set aside.

2. Remove the stems from the spinach and tear the leaves into small pieces. Mix the spinach and greens in a bowl. Arrange heaps of the salad mixture on 8 plates. Cut approximately ½ inch off the top of each pear, core and slice into ⅛-inch slices. Arrange 3–4 slices of pear on top of each plate of salad greens. Scatter the cheese and walnuts on top.

3. Place the port in a small saucepan over medium-high heat and cook until it has reduced by half. Stir in the sugar until dissolved. Remove the pan from the heat, stir in the balsamic vinegar and slowly whisk in the olive oil.

4. While the mixture is still warm, drizzle it over each salad. Lightly season with freshly ground pepper if desired.

SERVES 8

## HINZERLING WINERY

1520 Sheridan Avenue, Prosser
TEL: (509) 786-2163 or
1 (800) 727-6702
www.hinzerling.com
info@hinzerling.com

### WINE SHOP, TOURS AND TASTINGS
Open Mar.–Christmas, Mon.–Sat.
11 a.m.–5 p.m. and Sun. 11 a.m.–4 p.m.
Closed Sun. during winter except on
holiday weekends.

### GETTING THERE
From I-82 westbound take Exit 82.
Turn left onto Wine Country Road
and continue until you reach the
winery at Sheridan Avenue. From
I-82 eastbound take Exit 80. Turn
right onto Wine Country Road. Past
the bridge, the road forks. Take the
left fork, and continue on Wine
Country Road until you reach the
winery at Sheridan Avenue.

### WINERY HIGHLIGHTS
Come and visit Vintner's Inn at
Hinzerling Winery, a small country
inn dedicated to the enjoyment
of Yakima Valley food, wines and
microbrews.

# Organic Greens with Toasted Pine Nuts and Blackberry Vinaigrette

*featuring* BLACKBERRY WINE

¾ cup blackberry wine

1 small shallot, diced

1 Tbsp sugar

¼ cup apple cider vinegar

1 Tbsp Dijon mustard

½ cup canola oil

½ cup pine nuts

12 cups mixed organic greens

½ cup crumbled feta cheese

*The Greeks have been including feta cheese in their salads for an eternity, but here in North America the trend did not catch on until the 1970s. This delicious salad has that wonderful mixture of salty and sweet as well as the exciting texture contrasts of the pine nuts and soft cheese. Use a different fruit wine for a completely different, yet equally delicious result.*

1. Combine the blackberry wine, shallot and sugar in a small saucepan over medium heat. Bring to a boil, then reduce the heat and simmer for 15 minutes.

2. Transfer the mixture to a food processor or blender and add the vinegar and mustard. While blending, slowly add the canola oil.

3. Place the pine nuts in a dry pan over medium heat. Stir frequently until lightly toasted, making sure not to burn them.

4. Divide the greens evenly among the plates. Top with the desired amount of dressing and sprinkle with pine nuts and crumbled feta cheese.

SERVES 4–6

# Caesar Salad with Goat Cheese Croutons

Many people associate this salad with Julius Caesar, the Roman emperor; however, it's actually named after César Cardini, a restaurateur from Tijuana, Mexico. The salad was created during the 1920s and since then it has achieved worldwide fame. During the 1990s a law in California made the use of raw egg in food illegal, so for a while this salad was off the menu. The law was soon changed and the salad is no longer banned there. This version replaces the traditional croutons with crumbed goat cheese. We think you will approve.

1 egg at room temperature

4 cloves garlic

⅓ cup white wine

1 Tbsp lemon juice

2 tsp Worcestershire sauce

8 anchovy fillets, 4 chopped and 4 whole

1 tsp dried mustard

¼ tsp salt

¾ cup extra virgin olive oil

1 log goat cheese (4 oz)

½ cup fine breadcrumbs

1 large head romaine lettuce, torn into bite-sized pieces

1 Tbsp butter

*1.* Separate the egg yolk from the white and reserve the white for later use. Mix the yolk, garlic, wine, lemon juice, Worcestershire sauce, 4 whole anchovy fillets, dry mustard and salt in a food processor or blender. Process until smooth. Continue to blend while adding the olive oil in a slow stream, reserving 1 Tbsp. Transfer the mixture to a small bowl and add the chopped anchovies. If you find the mixture is too thick, add some more wine to thin it. Mix well, cover and refrigerate for 1–2 hours.

*2.* Cut the goat cheese log into ¼-inch-thick slices. Put the breadcrumbs on a small plate. Coat each cheese slice in the reserved egg white and then the breadcrumbs. Set the crumbed cheese slices on a small plate until you are ready to cook.

*3.* Toss the lettuce with the dressing and distribute evenly among the plates.

*4.* Heat the remaining 1 Tbsp of oil and the butter in a small pan over medium heat until the butter has melted. Sauté the cheese slices for about 1–2 minutes on each side or until light brown on the outside and creamy in the middle. Transfer the cooked cheese slices to the individual salads and serve immediately.

SERVES 4–6

# Soups & Stews

Well, dinner would have been splendid if the
wine had been as cold as the soup, the beef as
rare as the service, the brandy as old as the fish
and the maid as willing as the Duchess.

—*Winston Churchill*

# Isenhower Cellars Butternut Squash Soup with Pesto

*featuring* Isenhower Cellars Columbia Valley Snapdragon

2 medium butternut squash

2 Tbsp unsalted butter

2 medium leeks (white parts only), thinly sliced

1 small sweet onion (Walla Walla), chopped

1 Tbsp chopped fresh ginger

1 lime, juiced

3 cups chicken stock

1 cup dry white wine

kosher salt and freshly ground black pepper to taste

¼ cup coarsely grated Gruyère cheese

2 Tbsp toasted pine nuts, coarsely chopped

¼ cup packed fresh basil leaves, finely chopped

1 Tbsp grated Pamigiano Reggiano

3 slices cooked bacon, chopped

*A blending accident in 2002 led to the creation of this unique Washington white wine, which is 55 percent Roussanne and 45 percent Viognier. Roussanne has flavors of mango, orange peel and nutmeg. Viognier adds flavors of peach, apricot and bananas. Partial fermentation in new French oak barrels adds a layer of cream. The Snapdragon is food friendly and is an ideal match for this soup. It also goes well with shellfish, as well as Creole and Thai cuisine.*

*1.* Preheat the oven to 375°F. Halve each squash lengthwise, scoop out the seeds and arrange cut side down on a lightly oiled baking sheet. Bake for 50–60 minutes, until very tender, then cool to room temperature. When cool enough to handle, scrape out the pulp.

*2.* Heat the butter in a large soup pot over medium heat. Add the leeks, onion, ginger and lime juice and cook for about 5 minutes, stirring often, until softened. Add the squash, chicken stock and wine.

*3.* Increase the heat to high and bring to a boil. Reduce the heat to medium-high and simmer for about 10 minutes, stirring often, until the leeks are tender. Working in batches, purée the soup in a food processor or blender until smooth. Thin with additional stock as needed to reach the desired consistency. Return to the soup pot and season with salt and pepper.

**ISENHOWER CELLARS**

3471 Pranger Road, Walla Walla

TEL: (509) 526-7896

FAX: (509) 525-8118

www.isenhowercellars.com

info@isenhowercellars.com

WINE SHOP, TOURS AND TASTINGS
Open weekends 10:30 a.m. to 5 p.m.
Tasting is free and fun is guaranteed.

GETTING THERE
Isenhower Cellars is on the south
side of Walla Walla, 1 mile east of
Highway 125 on the corner of the Old
Milton Highway and Pranger Road.

WINERY HIGHLIGHTS
This is a small, family-owned winery
specializing in Rhône-style wines
and in single-vineyard Cabernet
Sauvignon that captures the essence
of the vineyards.

4. To prepare the pesto, combine the Gruyère, pine nuts, basil, Parmigiano Reggiano and bacon in a small bowl. Season to taste with salt and pepper. Keep at room temperature until ready to serve.

5. Serve the soup in warmed bowls. Garnish with a spoonful of pesto just before serving.

SERVES 8

# French Onion Soup

3 Tbsp butter

3 Tbsp olive oil

1½ lb onions, thinly sliced

4 cloves garlic, crushed

1 bay leaf

1 sprig thyme

1 tsp sugar

1 cup dry white wine

6 cups beef stock

4–6 slices sourdough bread

1 cup grated Gruyère cheese

½ cup grated Parmesan cheese

salt and freshly ground black pepper to taste

*The trick to making great French onion soup is to cook the onions for a long time over low heat so they caramelize. This recipe is simple, yet authentic, and will produce excellent results every time.*

1. Melt the butter with 1 Tbsp of the oil in a saucepan over medium heat. Add the onions, 2 of the crushed garlic cloves, bay leaf, thyme and sugar. Stir and cook for about 5 minutes, until the onions just begin to brown. Reduce the heat to medium-low and let the onions cook for another 30 minutes, stirring every 10 minutes or so.

2. Add the wine to deglaze the pan and use a wooden spoon to scrape up all the brown caramelized bits from the bottom. Add the beef stock and increase the heat to bring back to a boil. Turn the heat down to a very low simmer and cook uncovered for about 45 minutes.

3. Meanwhile, combine the remaining 2 crushed cloves of garlic and 2 Tbsp olive oil in a small bowl. Brush this mixture over the sourdough and toast under the broiler. When 1 side is done, flip it and repeat. When the soup is ready, cover the toast with a mixture of the 2 cheeses and broil again until the cheese melts.

4. Remove the bay leaf and thyme sprig from the soup and discard. Season with salt and pepper and ladle the soup into individual bowls. Place a cheese toast on the top of each bowl of soup and serve. Congratulations, you have just made classic French onion soup!

SERVES 4–6

# Cioppino

*This is a dish that's guaranteed to become a family favorite. My mother-in-law makes it and I will drive for hours to visit upon the mere suggestion that it might be served. Substitute any fresh vegetables or seafood you have available.*

1. Heat the olive oil in a large pot over medium-high heat and add the onion, green peppers, celery, carrot and garlic. Sauté for about 6–7 minutes, until soft. Add the tomatoes, tomato sauce, basil, marjoram, bay leaf and parsley, and bring to a boil. Reduce the heat, cover and allow to simmer for 2 hours. Discard the bay leaf.

2. Add the wine, fish, prawns and scallops to the sauce and simmer covered for about 10 minutes.

3. Discard any mussels that have damaged shells or mussels that will not close when you tap them gently against the countertop. Scrub mussels to remove barnacles and remove the beards by tearing them out of the shell. Rinse under clean running water. Add the mussels and cover the pot, allowing them to steam for about 7 minutes, or until the shells are fully open. Remove and discard any unopened mussels.

4. Serve this seafood stew with crusty bread and the same dry white wine you used in the recipe.

3 Tbsp olive oil

1 large onion, chopped

2 green bell peppers, chopped

2 stalks celery, chopped

1 carrot, chopped

4 cloves garlic, crushed

2 cans chopped tomatoes (16 oz each)

1 can tomato sauce (8 oz)

1 tsp dried basil

1 tsp dried marjoram

1 bay leaf

¼ cup chopped fresh flat-leaf parsley

½ cup dry white wine

1 lb boneless halibut, cut in small pieces

1 lb prawns, peeled and deveined

1 lb scallops

1 lb live mussels

salt and freshly ground black pepper to taste

# Swiss Broccoli Soup

*featuring* RIESLING

2½ lb broccoli

¼ cup butter

1 cup chopped leeks

¼ cup all-purpose flour

3½ cups chicken stock
(vegetarians can use
vegetable stock)

½ cup Riesling

1 cup light cream

1 cup shredded Swiss cheese

⅛ tsp nutmeg

salt and freshly ground black
pepper to taste

*Broccoli is one of our all-time favorite vegetables and we love this recipe from Ellena Conway of Latah Creek Winery. The cheese, leeks and wine all work together to give this simple soup a complex and very sophisticated taste. This recipe was made using the Latah Creek Riesling.*

1. Cut 2 cups of 1-inch broccoli florets. Cut the rest of the broccoli into 1-inch pieces and steam all the broccoli over boiling water for 5–6 minutes or until just tender. Rinse under cold water to stop further cooking. Set the 2 cups of steamed florets aside for later use.

2. Melt the butter in a medium saucepan over medium-high heat. Add the leeks and sauté for about 4–5 minutes until tender. Sprinkle in the flour and stir for another minute before removing from the heat.

3. Stir the stock and wine into the leek mixture, return to the heat and bring to a simmer. Allow to simmer for 5 minutes. Add the broccoli pieces (not the reserved florets) to the mix.

4. Purée the soup until smooth in a blender or food processor (you may have to do this in batches) and return to the pot over a low heat. Stir in the cream, cheese and nutmeg and simmer until the cheese melts. Add the reserved broccoli florets and allow them to heat through.

5. Season with salt and pepper and serve immediately.

SERVES 6–8

# Turkey Soup

*Leftover turkey? This soup makes a nice change from turkey sandwiches. Those who favor a health kick after the holidays will appreciate that it's full of good ingredients. You'll wish you'd made a bigger batch.*

1. Melt the butter in a large soup pot over medium-high heat. Add the celery, carrots, onions and garlic and sauté for 5–6 minutes or until the vegetables are softened.

2. Add the turnip, rice, stock and bay leaf and bring to a boil. Reduce the heat to a simmer, cover and simmer for 40 minutes.

3. Add the wine, turkey, mushrooms, lemon juice and onion powder and simmer for an additional 5 minutes. Season with salt and pepper.

4. Remove the bay leaf before serving. This soup is best served with a loaf of crusty bread.

SERVES 4

## CHEF'S TIP

*Here's an easy way to make 7 cups of turkey stock. Put the turkey bones and any leftover skin in a large pot and add 16 cups of water. Add 3 stalks chopped celery, 3 chopped carrots, 2 quartered onions, 2 Tbsp parsley, 1 Tbsp peppercorns and 1 tsp dried thyme. Bring to a boil and then reduce the heat to a simmer. It will take about 4 hours for the stock to reduce to 7 cups. Strain through a fine sieve or cheesecloth and discard the solids. Refrigerate the stock for a few hours, then scrape off and discard any fat. You can use the stock immediately or freeze it for later use.*

3 Tbsp butter

1½ cups diced celery

1½ cups chopped carrots

1½ cups chopped onions

2 cloves garlic, crushed

1½ cups diced turnip

1 cup wild rice

7 cups turkey stock (or chicken stock)

1 bay leaf

1 cup Pinot Blanc

2½ cups cooked diced turkey

1 cup sliced fresh mushrooms

1 Tbsp lemon juice

1 Tbsp onion powder

salt and freshly ground black pepper to taste

*Soups & Stews*  43

# JLC Winery's Spofford Station Cabernet Cowbourguignon

*featuring* SPOFFORD STATION CABERNET SAUVIGNON

6 oz thick-cut streaky bacon, cut in thin strips

3½ lb top round steak, cut in pieces

3 Tbsp butter

12 oz baby onions

12 oz button mushrooms

1 sweet onion (Walla Walla), finely chopped

12 oz baby carrots

4 cloves garlic, crushed

3 Tbsp all-purpose flour

3 cups Cabernet Sauvignon

3 cups beef stock

3 Tbsp tomato purée

1 Tbsp chopped fresh parsley

salt and freshly ground black pepper to taste

*Cabernet is the workhorse of the winery. This is a full-bodied and complex wine, with explosive fruits, ginger and a hint of mint. (Could it be from the farm's mint crop adjacent to the vineyard row?) Winemaker and farmer J.L. Chamberlain uses the pomace (pressed grapes) to feed the cattle. These unique cows fed on grape skins are becoming known throughout the world as "Cabernet Cows." We recommend using Cabernet Cow meat for this recipe if you can get your hands on some.*

*1.* Cook the bacon in a large pan over medium heat for about 5–7 minutes, until golden brown. Remove the bacon from the pan and drain on paper towel. Pour out all but 2 Tbsp of the bacon fat.

*2.* Increase the heat to medium-high. Working in batches, add the beef in a single layer; do not crowd the pan. Brown the meat on all sides, about 5–6 minutes. Transfer the browned meat to a plate and continue until all the beef is browned.

*3.* Add 1 Tbsp of the butter and reduce the heat to medium. Add the baby onions and stir until golden, then set them aside. In the same pan melt 1 Tbsp of the remaining butter and sauté the mushrooms for 4–5 minutes, until golden. Set them aside with the onions.

## JLC WINERY
16 North 2nd Street, Walla Walla
TEL: (509) 529-1398
FAX: (509) 529-1426
www.jamesleighcellars.com
info@jamesleighcellars.com

### WINE SHOP, TOURS AND TASTINGS
Open weekends and by appointment.
They love guests, so just call ahead
to make an appointment.

### GETTING THERE
Located 3 blocks from the main
downtown exit to Walla Walla on
2nd Street.

### WINERY HIGHLIGHTS
JLC Winery and Spofford Station
feature ultra-premium estate wines.
They strive for well-balanced and
elegant Bordeaux-type wines done in
Walla Walla style.

### WINERY SPECIAL OFFER
If you show your copy of this book,
you will receive a free tasting and any
bottles purchased will be signed for
you. Your name will go into a draw for
a Cabernet Cow dinner!

**4.** Remove any excess fat from the pan. Melt the last Tbsp of butter and sauté the sweet onion, carrots and garlic. Cook for about 5 minutes, until softened. Sprinkle with the flour, add the wine, beef stock and tomato purée and bring to a boil.

**5.** Transfer everything except the mushrooms and baby onions to a slow cooker. Cook on low heat for 6–8 hours (or use a covered casserole dish in the oven at 325°F for 3½–4½ hours) until the meat is fork-tender. Add the baby onions and mushrooms for the last 45 minutes of cooking. Garnish with parsley, season with salt and pepper and serve.

SERVES 6–8

# Mushroom and Pinot Noir Soup

*featuring* Pinot Noir

3 Tbsp butter

2 shallots, finely chopped

2 cloves garlic, crushed

1 lb mixed mushrooms, chopped (slice a couple for garnish)

1 cup Pinot Noir

4 cups stock (vegetable, mushroom or chicken)

1 cup whipping cream

2 Tbsp chopped fresh parsley, for garnish

*One of the all-time greatest wine pairings for mushrooms is Pinot Noir. In this soup the deep, earthy flavors of the mushrooms and the Pinot Noir complement each other beautifully.*

1. Melt 1 Tbsp of the butter in a large saucepan over medium heat. Add the shallots and garlic and sauté for 1–2 minutes. Add the remaining 2 Tbsp butter and the chopped mushrooms and cook for about 5 minutes, until they begin to soften. You may need to add more butter as the mushrooms absorb it very quickly.

2. Add the wine and cook for 5 minutes, allowing the wine to reduce. Add the stock and increase the heat to a boil. Reduce the heat and allow to simmer for 20 minutes. Remove the pot from the heat and allow it to cool.

3. When the soup has cooled slightly, purée it in a blender or food processor. You may have to do this in batches. Return the puréed mixture to the pot over low heat. Stir in the cream and allow it to heat through without letting it boil.

4. Serve in individual bowls garnished with the reserved sliced mushrooms and chopped parsley.

Serves 6

# Pinot Noir

*pronounced* (PEE-NO-NWAHR)

*The Pinot Noir grape has been used to make wine since at least the first century AD. Ancient Romans called the grape* **Helvenacia Minor.** *The grape is most famous because of the wines produced in the Burgundy region of France; however, many wine experts claim that the world's best Pinot Noir comes from the Pacific Northwest.*

*Pinot Noir is known as one of the toughest grapes to grow and to turn into wine, and it has not achieved the popularity of some other reds because its overall quality is generally a little more inconsistent. The 2004 film* **Sideways** *has boosted Pinot Noir sales, and when it is done right Pinot Noir is many wine lovers' favorite tipple.*

*There is very little Pinot Noir grown in Washington; the majority of US Pinot Noir comes from south of the Washington/Oregon border. But there are still some great examples of the wine being produced here. The Columbia Gorge region, in particular, has an excellent climate for these grapes.*

*Pinot Noir can have many different characteristics, but some common ones include flavors and aromas of raspberry, cherry, rose petals, oregano and rhubarb. The wine is generally believed to be at its best five to eight years after the vintage.*

*This wine is wonderful with a wide variety of foods. Some fabulous pairings are salmon, tuna, lamb, chicken, pork, smoked meats, hearty stews, wild mushrooms and duck.*

# Real Corn Chowder

4 ears fresh corn

2½ cups chicken stock (or vegetable stock)

2½ cups whipping cream

4 oz butter

2 shallots, diced

2 cloves garlic, crushed

1 green bell pepper, diced

2 stalks celery, chopped

2 carrots, chopped

2 Tbsp all-purpose flour

½ cup dry white wine

2 medium red potatoes, cubed

salt and freshly ground black pepper to taste

*Corn is the number-one field crop in the United States. If you're in the Snohomish River Valley area in the fall, keep an eye out for Washington's biggest corn maze at "The Farm." This delicious corn chowder will have you pining for the fall corn crop year-round.*

1. Peel the corn and remove all the kernels from the cob with a sharp knife. Set the kernels aside. Bring the stock and cream to a simmer in a large pan and add the bare corn cobs. Ensure the heat is very low and let the cobs simmer in the cream mixture for about 45 minutes. Remove the mixture from the heat and discard the cobs.

2. Meanwhile, melt the butter in a sauté pan over medium-high heat and add the corn kernels, shallots, garlic, green pepper, celery and carrots. Cook for 6–7 minutes, until they begin to soften. Add the flour and stir through well. After 1 minute, add the wine and continue to stir for about 2 minutes, allowing the wine to reduce.

3. Add the cream mixture and the potatoes. Bring to a simmer, but do not let the mixture boil. After 12–15 minutes the potatoes should be tender. Season with salt and pepper and serve.

SERVES 4

Gordon Brothers vineyard overlooks the Snake River in the Columbia Valley  (page 29)
PREVIOUS PAGE:  Domaine Ste. Michelle Tempura-Battered Halibut with Dipping Sauce  (page 16)

The cattle feed on grape skins at JLC Winery. These cows are known as "Cabernet Cows." (page 44)

A picnic at Chateau Ste. Michelle  (page 97)  KEVIN KRUFF PHOTO

OPPOSITE:  Hinzerling's Pear, Port, Cheese and Walnut Salad  (page 32)

The magnificent Arbor Crest Winery (page 77) PHOTO COURTESY OF ARBOR CREST WINERY
OPPOSITE: Isenhower Cellars Butternut Squash Soup with Pesto (page 38)
NEXT PAGE: Tagaris Cast Iron King Salmon with Syrah Drizzle (page 70)

# Ribollita

This Tuscan vegetable soup recipe comes from La Toscana Winery and was originally made using their Rosso Rustico red wine. Ribollita is Italian for "re-boiled" or "re-cooked." They say that although it's great to eat immediately, it's even better the next day when it's re-boiled. We doubt you'll have any leftovers though.

1. Purée 2 cans of the beans in a blender or food processor and set aside.

2. Heat the oil in a large pot over medium heat. Add the onions and garlic and sauté for 3–4 minutes or until soft. Add the carrots, celery, potatoes, Swiss chard, kale and cabbage and mix well. Add the tomatoes and 1 cup of the chicken stock, cover and allow to cook for about 20 minutes or until the greens wilt.

3. Add the remaining 7 cups chicken stock and the puréed beans and mix well. Simmer over low heat for 1 hour. Add the remaining can of beans and the 3 slices of country bread, crumbling it into the soup. Add the wine and allow it to simmer for another 4–5 minutes. Season with salt and pepper.

4. To serve, place cubed white bread in the bottom of each bowl and sprinkle with Parmigiano Reggiano. Ladle the soup over the bread cubes and sprinkle with more cheese if desired or drizzle with some olive oil. *Buon appetito!*

SERVES 6

3 cans cannellini beans (14 oz each)

¼ cup extra virgin olive oil

2 medium yellow onions, chopped

2 cloves garlic, crushed

2 carrots, peeled and sliced

2 stalks celery, strings removed, sliced

2 large potatoes, peeled and chunked

1 large bunch Swiss chard, trimmed and chopped

1 bunch kale, trimmed and chopped

1 small Savoy cabbage, trimmed and chopped

1 cup canned Italian plum tomatoes, sliced

8 cups chicken stock (use more or less depending on how much broth you want)

3 thick slices day-old country bread

¾ cup red wine

salt and freshly ground black pepper to taste

3 slices white day-old bread, cubed

½ cup grated Parmigiano Reggiano

# Fish & Seafood

Red wine with fish! Well, that should
have told me something!

—*James Bond in* From Russia with Love *after he is
deceived by an undercover Russian agent*

# Carpenter Creek's Simple Seafood Spaghetti

*featuring* CARPENTER CREEK CHARDONNAY

3 Tbsp olive oil

1 Tbsp salt

1½ lb thin spaghetti

5 cloves garlic, crushed

1 lb shrimp, peeled

1 lb crabmeat (imitation is ok
but real is better!)

¼ cup Chardonnay

4 ripe Roma tomatoes,
chopped

1 bunch fresh basil, roughly
chopped

14 oz feta cheese, crumbled

salt and freshly ground black
pepper to taste

*This recipe is very quick to prepare and the results are magnificent. The Chardonnay is crisp and dry, with intense varietal flavors that complement the seafood. Buttery oak and subtle vanillin notes from 10 months of oak aging give it depth and complexity. Malolactic (secondary) fermentation and sur lie aging (leaving the wine to age on the lees of the first fermentation) add to the richness of this wine.*

*1.* Bring a large pot of water to a boil. When the water boils add 1 Tbsp of the olive oil, salt and spaghetti. Boil for 6 minutes, then drain the pasta.

*2.* Heat the remaining 2 Tbsp olive oil until fragrant in a large pan over high heat and sauté the garlic for 1 minute. Add the shrimp and crab and sauté briefly, about 1 minute. Add the wine and cook down briefly, 1–2 minutes. Lower the heat, add the tomatoes, basil and feta and bring to a simmer. Season with salt and pepper.

*3.* Add half the sauce to the pasta and stir well. Divide the pasta among the serving plates and top with the remainder of the sauce. Enjoy another glass of wine with your dinner!

SERVES 6–8

## CARPENTER CREEK WINERY

20376 East Hickox Road
Mount Vernon
TEL: (360) 848-6673 or
1 (866) WA-WINES
FAX: (815) 572-9267
www.carpentercreek.com
info@carpentercreek.com

### WINE SHOP, TOURS AND TASTINGS

Gift shop and tasting room open
Fri.-Sat. 10 a.m.–6 p.m. and by
appointment.

### GETTING THERE

From I-5 take Andersons Road exit
255 (coming from the north you turn
left and cross the freeway, coming
from the south you turn right). Take
the first right onto Cedardale Road
and follow for 1 mile to Hickox Road.
Turn left on Hickox Road and follow it
for 1 mile to the end of the road. It is
the last driveway on the right.

### WINERY HIGHLIGHTS

Nestled among tall pines and cedar
groves, with its namesake gently
burbling in the background, this is
an idyllic place to sample fine wines,
enjoy a winery tour or event, or
simply to picnic along the beautiful
shores of the creek.

### WINERY SPECIAL OFFER

If you show your copy of this
book you'll receive a free souvenir
wineglass with your tasting!

# Baked Whole Salmon

*featuring* SAUVIGNON BLANC

1 salmon, cleaned and scaled (4–5 lb)

1 Tbsp seasoning salt

1 lemon, halved

10 whole peppercorns

½ cup chopped green onions

2 bay leaves

¼ cup chopped flat-leaf parsley

½ cup Sauvignon Blanc

*There is something really satisfying about baking a whole fish, but if your oven is not big enough, it's off with its head! There are five species of Pacific Northwest salmon: chinook, coho, pink, sockeye and chum. Sea-run cutthroat trout and steelhead are also from the salmonid family; however, they are not generally recognized as being salmon. All the species mentioned could be used for this dish, although we've never tried it with chum.*

1. Preheat the oven to 350°F. Cut 2 sheets of aluminum foil a few inches longer than your fish and place on a large baking sheet (doubling the foil prevents tearing). Put the fish on the foil and fold up the edges of the foil to make a tray with sides.

2. Rub the inside of the salmon with the seasoning salt. Squeeze 1 lemon half over the fish. Slice the remaining half and arrange the slices in the cavity of the fish. Arrange the peppercorns, green onions, bay leaves and parsley inside the fish. Add the wine and then wrap the foil around the fish and seal carefully to avoid losing the liquid.

3. Transfer the fish to the oven and bake for 40 minutes. Turn off the oven but do not open the door. Let the fish cook inside the warm oven for another 40 minutes.

4. When you open the foil you should easily be able to remove the skin from the top of the fish. Flip it over and remove the skin from the other side. You can serve the salmon hot or cold. You can even bake the fish the day before, cover and refrigerate. Serve garnished with fresh lemons and parsley.

SERVES 6–8

# Poached Salmon with Creamy Chive Sauce

*Chives not only taste good, but also look very attractive in a sauce. Home gardeners should know that it's possible to eat the chive flowers as well, and they make a stunning garnish. The only concern is that as the plant flowers the onion flavor of the leaves becomes a lot more intense.*

1½ cups white wine

½ cup water

1 clove garlic, crushed

1 small onion, thickly sliced

4 lemon slices

1 tsp salt

4 salmon fillets (6 oz each)

3 Tbsp butter

3 Tbsp all-purpose flour

¼ cup whipping cream

salt and freshly ground black pepper to taste

¼ cup chopped fresh chives

1. Combine the wine, water, garlic, onion, lemon slices and salt in a pan deep enough to fully immerse the salmon fillets. Bring to a boil and place the salmon in the pan. There should be just enough liquid to cover the fish. If necessary, add additional water or wine. When the liquid returns to a boil, reduce the heat to low, cover and simmer for about 10 minutes or until the fish flakes with a fork.

2. Remove the cooked fish from the pan immediately with a slotted spatula and keep warm. Strain the poaching liquid and set aside.

3. Melt the butter in a small saucepan over medium heat. Stir in the flour until well combined. Measure out 1½ cups of the poaching liquid and add it a little at a time, stirring quickly. Once the poaching liquid has been added and the sauce is thick, add the cream and season with salt and pepper. Add the chives just before serving and stir well.

4. Serve the salmon topped with the chive sauce, and accompany with boiled baby potatoes. There will be plenty of sauce to serve on the potatoes as well!

SERVES 4

# Crutcher Cellars Shrimp Etouffée

*featuring* CRUTCHER CELLARS WASHINGTON STATE VIOGNIER

½ cup unsalted butter

¼ cup all-purpose flour

2 cups chopped yellow onions

1 cup chopped celery

1 cup chopped green bell
    pepper

½ tsp salt

¼ tsp freshly ground black
    pepper

3 tsp minced garlic

1 jalapeño (or serrano) pepper
    seeds removed, minced

1 can chopped tomatoes
    (14 oz)

1 cup Viognier

1 Tbsp Cajun seasoning

1½ lb shrimp, peeled and
    deveined

4 green onions, green parts
    only, chopped

⅓ cup chopped fresh parsley

*Rich Altice has created this exciting recipe that shows off the harmonious pairing of wine and shrimp. Crutcher Cellars is very excited about its Washington State Viognier, as this wine was its first major bottling. It shows generous pear, peach and pineapple on the nose and follows with bright tropical fruit flavors with a crisp, clean finish. This is an excellent food wine but is also wonderful on its own on a warm summer evening.*

*1.* Melt the butter in a frying pan over medium-high heat. Add the flour and stir to form a roux. Cook until it's the color of peanut butter.

*2.* Add the yellow onion, celery, green pepper, salt and pepper and cook for about 5 minutes, until the onions are translucent. Add the garlic and jalapeño pepper and cook for an additional minute. Add the tomatoes with their juice, wine and Cajun seasoning. Cover and simmer for 10 minutes.

*3.* Add the shrimp and cook just until they turn pink, about 3–4 minutes. Add the green onion and parsley and cook for an additional 2 minutes.

*4.* Serve over steamed rice with plenty of French bread.

*5.* Accompany with a glass of Crutcher Cellars Washington State Viognier.

SERVES 6

## CRUTCHER CELLARS

24707 SE 45th Place, Issaquah

TEL: (425) 417-0115

www.crutchercellars.com

info@crutchercellars.com

WINE SHOP, TOURS AND TASTINGS

Tasting by appointment only.

GETTING THERE

Call ahead for directions.

WINERY HIGHLIGHTS

Crutcher Cellars is one of the new generation of wineries in Washington State. Their initial crush in 2004 will produce less than 500 cases and they expect production to peak at less than 2,000 cases per year. Their goal is to produce small lots of exceptional wine that show the best of what Washington can produce.

# Viognier

*pronounced (VEE-OHN-YAY)*

*Viognier is back with a vengeance! This white Rhone Valley varietal was almost wiped out during the 1960s when it was reduced to just a few acres. Then Viognier fans began to spread the news about how wonderful this wine was, and it seems that the world listened.*

*The grape dates back to the times of the Roman Empire; some historians place it as early as AD 280. Well over 1,000 years later, in the late 1980s, the grape was brought to America. More Viognier is grown in the United States than in any other country in the world, although the grape is now grown in Brazil, Australia and even Japan. Today it is commonly known as Washington's rising star and some think it has the potential to rival Chardonnay in popularity. Viognier is usually made into a dry-style wine and it has proved to be particularly appealing to Chardonnay drinkers, who are rapidly becoming Viognier converts.*

*Some common characteristics of the wine include a rich and very distinctive aroma that might be described as a mix of tropical fruits and citrus blossoms. It has a creamy mouth feel that is common in oak-aged Chardonnays.*

*Viognier is delightful with spicy dishes, especially Thai and Mexican food. It also pairs well with aged cheeses, pork, fish, chicken and poached fruit.*

# Eleven Winery's Lemon Pepper Baked Flounder

*featuring* ELEVEN WINERY SAUVIGNON BLANC

**2 Tbsp grated lemon rind**

**2 cloves garlic, minced**

**4 flounder fillets (6 oz each)**

**1 Tbsp olive oil (or cooking spray)**

**1¼ tsp freshly ground black pepper**

**½ tsp salt**

**½ cup Sauvignon Blanc**

**2 Tbsp butter**

**lemon wedges**

*Eleven Winery makes Sauvignon Blanc the way it should be: crisp and refreshing, with a clean, dry finish. With citrus on the nose, it is a mouthful of tart apple and more citrus, with mineral, floral and herbal undertones—a perfect accompaniment to the lemon in this recipe. Note that in some supermarkets flounder is sold as sole.*

*1.* Preheat the oven to 425°F. In a small bowl combine the lemon rind and garlic.

*2.* Place the flounder in a cast iron pan or other ovenproof pan greased with the oil. Rub the garlic mixture over the fillets and sprinkle with the pepper and salt. Bake for about 8 minutes or until the fish flakes easily with a fork. Remove the fish from the pan and keep warm.

*3.* Add the wine to the pan over medium-high heat and deglaze, making sure to scrape up the brown bits from the bottom. Add the butter to the pan and boil until reduced by half, about 4 minutes.

*4.* Serve the fish with the sauce and lemon wedges on the side. Steamed asparagus makes a tasty accompaniment.

SERVES 4

**ELEVEN WINERY**

12976 Roe Road NE
Bainbridge Island
TEL: (206) 780-0905
www.elevenwinery.com
info@elevenwinery.com

WINE SHOP, TOURS AND TASTINGS
Call or email anytime to arrange
a tasting appointment.

GETTING THERE
Contact the winery for an
appointment and they'll supply
directions.

WINERY HIGHLIGHTS
Eleven Winery is a new, small,
family-run winery dedicated to
producing great wine.

WINERY SPECIAL OFFER
Show your copy of this book and
get 20 percent off a bottle of
Sauvignon Blanc.

# Hoodsport's Dosiwallips Scallops

*featuring* HOODSPORT SAUVIGNON BLANC

½ cup Sauvignon Blanc

½ cup chicken stock

1 Tbsp Dijon mustard

2 Tbsp butter

2 Tbsp olive oil

1 lb scallops

¼ cup all-purpose flour

¼ cup whipping cream

*This bright and lively wine has aromas and flavors of grapefruit and pear and finishes with balanced acidity. It's an excellent example of the essence of Sauvignon Blanc in the Pacific Northwest and is the perfect wine for delicate seafood like scallops.*

*1.* Combine the wine and stock in a saucepan. Bring to a boil and stir in the mustard and whipping cream. Reduce the heat and simmer, stirring frequently, for about 15 minutes.

*2.* Heat the butter and oil in a frying pan over medium-high heat. Lightly coat the scallops with flour. Sauté the scallops for about 2 minutes or until slightly browned.

*3.* Remove the excess oil, then pour the cream sauce into the pan with the scallops. Simmer for an additional 5–10 minutes depending on the size of your scallops.

*4.* We recommend serving this over a small nest of cooked butterfly or corkscrew pasta. Enjoy with a glass of Hoodsport Sauvignon Blanc.

SERVES 4 OF US, 6 HEALTH NUTS OR 2 LOGGERS

## HOODSPORT WINERY

N23501 Highway 101, Hoodsport
TEL: (360) 877-9894
FAX: (360) 877-9508
www.hoodsport.com
wine@hoodsport.com

### WINE SHOP, TOURS AND TASTINGS

Tasting room open daily 10 a.m.–
6 p.m. There is no charge for tasting.

### GETTING THERE

The winery is located about 1 mile
south of Hoodsport on scenic
Highway 101 along the Hood Canal.
Your travel time from Tacoma is
about 2 hours and from the Seattle
area it will vary depending on your
choice of ferries and roads.

### WINERY HIGHLIGHTS

They have fabulous fruit and berry
wines as well as the traditional
grape wines. Be sure to sample wine
made from their famous local Belle
wine grape.

### WINERY SPECIAL OFFER

Show your copy of this book and get
20 percent off your wine purchase.

# Classic Belgian-Style Mussels

5 lb live mussels

1 Tbsp butter

1 Tbsp olive oil

1 onion, chopped

2 stalks celery, chopped

1 cup dry white wine

½ cup whipping cream

¼ cup chopped fresh flat-leaf parsley

salt and freshly ground black pepper to taste

*Moules et frites! In Belgium you would likely be served this dish with a side of french fries. As wonderful as that is, we find a good chunk of crusty bread is enough to keep us satisfied. But if you want french fries, don't let us discourage you—10 million Belgians can't be wrong.*

1. Discard any mussels that have damaged shells or that do not close when you tap them gently against the countertop. Scrub the mussels and remove the beards by tearing them out of the shell. Rinse under clean running water.

2. Heat the butter and oil in a large pot over high heat. Add the onion and celery and sauté for 2 minutes before adding the wine. Cover and bring to a boil, then add the mussels and quickly replace the lid so the mussels cook in the steam.

3. After 5 minutes remove all the opened mussels from the pot and place them in serving bowls. Give any closed mussels 1 more minute and if they have not opened, discard them.

4. Add the cream and parsley to the wine broth and mix well while bringing to a simmer. Season with salt and pepper. Pour the broth over the mussels and serve immediately. Make sure you have some crusty bread to mop up the juices!

SERVES 4

# Tuna Merlot

*Merlot pairs beautifully with tuna. This is another example of how the "white wine with fish" rule doesn't apply. The National Marine Fisheries Service estimates that every year around 20 million albacore tuna pass by the coast, and one of the best ways to catch one in Washington is a charter from Westport. Tuna is at its best served rare.*

4 Tbsp olive oil

1 Tbsp butter

1 onion, chopped

1 red bell pepper, finely chopped

3 cloves garlic, crushed

½ cup Merlot

2 cans chopped tomatoes (15 oz each)

4 Tbsp chopped fresh herbs (basil, oregano, chives, parsley, etc.)

6 tuna steaks (6 oz each)

salt and freshly ground black pepper to taste

1. Heat 2 Tbsp of the oil and the butter in a frying pan over medium-high heat. Add the onion, red pepper and garlic and sauté for about 3 minutes. Add the wine, tomatoes and 3 Tbsp of the fresh herbs and stir well. Simmer for 10–15 minutes, until the sauce begins to thicken.

2. Season the tuna steaks lightly with salt and pepper. Heat the remaining 2 Tbsp of oil in a separate frying pan over high heat. Sauté the steaks for 2 minutes, turn them and allow another 1–2 minutes for rare or 3–4 minutes for well done.

3. Pool some sauce on each serving plate and top with a tuna steak. Garnish with the remaining fresh herbs.

SERVES 6

# Illusion's Grilled Oysters with Pinot Gris Reduction and Spinach Slaw

*featuring* ILLUSION PINOT GRIS

¼ cup butter

6 cloves garlic, finely chopped

2 cups Pinot Gris

1 tsp parsley, chopped

¼ tsp hot red pepper flakes

2 Tbsp lemon juice

½ tsp salt

black pepper to taste

1 cup fresh spinach cut into thin ½-inch strips

1 cup green cabbage cut into thin ½-inch strips

2 Tbsp chopped fresh cilantro or parsley

2 Tbsp chopped red onion

2 Tbsp finely chopped jalapeño pepper, seeds removed

2 Tbsp chopped lemon zest

salt and freshly ground black pepper to taste

2 Tbsp mayonnaise

1 tsp white wine vinegar

12 large fresh Northwest oysters in the shell

*Illusion's Pinot Gris was produced from grapes grown on Harold and Janet Pleasant's vineyard near Benton City in Washington's Columbia Valley. The wine's intense fruit flavors and seductive aromas make it a perfect pairing with fresh seafood and spicy summer dishes.*

*1.* Melt the butter in a small saucepan over medium-high heat. Sauté the garlic for about 2 minutes. Add the Pinot Gris, parsley, red pepper flakes, lemon juice, ½ tsp salt and black pepper to taste. Bring to a boil and then reduce to a simmer. Simmer until the liquid is reduced by half, around 30 minutes.

*2.* Prepare the spinach slaw by combining the spinach and cabbage in a small mixing bowl. Add the cilantro or parsley, red onion, jalapeño pepper and lemon zest. Season with salt and pepper. In a small bowl combine the mayonnaise and vinegar. Add the mayonnaise to the slaw and mix with a fork just until the mayonnaise mixture holds the slaw together.

*3.* Shuck the oysters, loosen them from the shell and arrange on the half shell on a hot grill. When the oysters are heated through, 2–4 minutes, remove from the grill. The oysters can also be baked in an oven at 400°F for 5–10 minutes. Either way, do not overcook them!

*4.* Top the hot oysters with a heaping spoonful of the spinach slaw. Serve with garlic bread and a well-chilled glass of Illusion Pinot Gris. This recipe is also suitable for raw oysters on the half shell.

SERVES 2

## ILLUSION

32446 Morgan Drive, Black Diamond

TEL: (206) 261-1682

www.illusionwine.com

illusion@sprintmail.com

WINE SHOP, TOURS AND TASTINGS
The small Black Diamond facility is
not open to the public; however, the
new winemaking facility, vineyard
and tasting room in the Columbia
River Gorge area are scheduled to
open in 2007.

GETTING THERE
Check the website for details on the
new tasting room.

WINERY HIGHLIGHTS
Founded in 2002 by Dave and Dina
Guest, Illusion is a small but growing
winery that produces only small lots
of premium red and white wines, all
from Washington State vineyards.

# AVA

*AVA stands for American Viticultural Area. These areas, or appellations, are designated and administered by the Alcohol Tobacco Tax and Trade Bureau (TTB). The system of AVAs is roughly based on the French system of* **Appellation d'Origine Contrôlée (AOC)** *with one huge difference.*

*AVAs are geographic boundaries only. The French appellation system offers a lot more information about what you can expect to find inside the bottle. The French AOC system provides information such as maximum yields, minimum sugar levels, time in oak, whether or not sugar has been added and more. In the United States, we are only given the broad geographic region where the grapes have been grown. The TTB has defined AVAs as "a delimited grape-growing region distinguishable by geographic features." These features refer to soil content, climate and general growing conditions that make the area unique.*

*There are around 100 AVAs in California alone, and more are being recognized all the time. In Washington (at the time of going to print) there are nine AVAs: Yakima Valley (1983), Walla Walla Valley (1984, shared with Oregon), Columbia Valley (1984, shared with Oregon), Puget Sound (1995), Red Mountain (2001), Columbia Gorge (2004, shared with Oregon), Horse Heaven Hills (2005), Wahluke Slope (2006) and Rattlesnake Hills (2006). It is expected this number will continue to increase, as there are more AVA applications pending.*

*If an AVA is listed on the label it is required by law that at least 85 percent of the grapes used to make the wine must have come from within that AVA.*

# Lost River's Creamy Prawn and Artichoke Lasagna

*featuring* LOST RIVER'S COLUMBIA VALLEY RAINSHADOW

1½ cups white wine

1½ lb raw prawns

¼ cup butter

⅓ cup finely chopped onion

2 cloves garlic, crushed

¼ cup all-purpose flour

¼ tsp cayenne pepper

1½ tsp paprika

½ tsp salt

1 cup whipping cream

1 lb ricotta cheese

2 eggs

1 cup finely grated Parmesan cheese

12 oz lasagna noodles, cooked (reserved in cold water)

12 oz canned artichoke hearts, drained and quartered

4 cups grated mozzarella and/or Jack cheese

*Lost River's Rainshadow is a blend of 40 percent Semillon and 60 percent Sauvignon Blanc grapes that come from 2 of Washington's finest white grape vineyards in the Yakima valley. The barrel-fermented Semillon adds a soft, nutty, citrus note that mingles magically with the creamy richness of this dish. The stainless steel–fermented Sauvignon Blanc adds crispness and bright fruit aromas that dance on the palate with the fresh flavors of prawns and artichokes.*

*1.* Bring the wine and ½ cup of water to a boil. Add the prawns and cook until they just turn pink. Remove the prawns from the broth and set the broth aside. When the prawns have cooled, remove the shells and cut the meat in half lengthwise. Set aside.

*2.* Heat the butter in a heavy saucepan over medium heat. Add the onion and garlic and cook for about 3 minutes or until transparent. Whisk in the flour and cook for a bit before adding the spices. Add the spices and salt and cook for 1 minute before slowly whisking in 1 cup of the reserved prawn broth and the cream. This should make a smooth, creamy sauce full of flavor.

*3.* Preheat the oven to 325°F. Combine the ricotta, eggs and Parmesan in a bowl. Add ⅔ of the sauce and mix well.

LOST RIVER WINERY
26 Highway 20, Winthrop
TEL: (509) 996-2888
FAX: (509) 996-2767
www.lostriverwinery.com
liam@lostriverwinery.com

WINE SHOP, TOURS AND TASTINGS
Open year-round Fri.–Sat. 11 a.m.–
5 p.m. Tastings and tours are free.

GETTING THERE
From Seattle travel east on I-90.
Exit at Cle Elum and follow the signs
to Wenatchee and Highway 2. At
Wenatchee take Highway 97 north
to Pateros. Travel north on Highway
153 and connect with Highway 20.
Travel through Winthrop to the
western edge of town. The winery
is on the right.

WINERY HIGHLIGHTS
Lost River's wines have won
numerous medals and are priced
for great value. A 10 percent case
discount is available.

4. Place $^1/_3$ of the cream sauce in a 9- x 13-inch baking dish. Add $^1/_3$ of the drained pasta, half the artichokes, half the prawns, half the ricotta filling and $^1/_3$ of the cheese. Repeat the layers, then finish with the remaining $^1/_3$ pasta, $^1/_3$ sauce and $^1/_3$ cheese. Bake the lasagna for about 30 minutes or until hot and bubbly.

5. The lasagna can be served immediately, but for best results cool to room temperature, cut into portions, cover and chill completely (overnight if possible). Bake for another 20 minutes at 350°F or until hot before serving. Serve with salad, crusty bread and a glass of Lost River's Rainshadow.

SERVES 6–8

# Garlic Prawns

*featuring* VIOGNIER

3 Tbsp butter

1 Tbsp olive oil

4 cloves garlic, crushed

1 lb raw prawns in the shell

⅓ cup Viognier

2 Tbsp chopped fresh parsley

*No one said cooking had to be difficult. Sometimes a few fresh ingredients thrown together in a pan is all you need. There is a lot of garlic in this recipe so it's best that everyone indulges. This is messy to eat, as you'll need to use your fingers to break into the prawns, but when you've worked for your meal it tastes even better!*

1. Melt the butter into the olive oil in a large frying pan over medium heat. When the oil is hot and the butter bubbling, add the garlic and prawns.

2. Allow the prawns to cook for about 3 minutes on each side. Add the wine and simmer for an additional 2 minutes.

3. Sprinkle the parsley overtop and serve with the remaining wine sauce. Accompany with rice, crusty bread, salad or even french fries. Supply a dish for shells; finger bowls with water and lemon slices are a great option. Enjoy with a glass of Viognier.

SERVES 2

# Clam Penne in White Wine

Washington has an abundance of clams, including the popular littleneck and Manila types. Although these species look very similar, only the littlenecks are native to the region. Manila clams came to Washington accidentally in oyster shipments from Japan. They have since flourished, which is great news for seafood lovers!

2–3 dozen live clams (littleneck or Manila)

14 oz penne

½ cup dry white wine

¼ cup extra virgin olive oil

4 cloves garlic, crushed

1 tsp red pepper flakes

1 red bell pepper, chopped

2 Tbsp chopped fresh parsley

sea salt and freshly ground black pepper to taste

1. Rinse the clams well under water to remove grit. Put the clams in a pot of cold salted water and let them sit for 15 minutes. If the clams expel grit, change the water and repeat the process; if not, just give the clams another rinse.

2. Cook the penne in a pot of salted water for about 8–10 minutes until it is *al dente*; there should be a slight resistance when you bite into it. Do not overcook. Drain the pasta and set aside.

3. Meanwhile, place the clams and wine in a large sauté pan over medium-high heat. Cover and simmer for 5 minutes, then remove any clams that have opened. Keep checking every couple of minutes until all the clams have opened and been removed. After 10 minutes remove the pan from the heat and discard any unopened clams.

4. Drain the liquid from the pan into a small bowl and wipe out any grit left in the pan. Return the liquid to the pan and add 2 Tbsp of the olive oil and the garlic, red pepper flakes and red pepper. Sauté for 3–4 minutes over medium-high heat. Add the drained pasta and clams to the pan and toss well. Add the chopped parsley, salt and pepper.

5. Divide among individual pasta bowls and drizzle with the remaining 2 Tbsp of olive oil. Set out a dish to collect the shells. Serve with a loaf of fresh crusty bread.

SERVES 4

# Tagaris Cast Iron King Salmon with Syrah Drizzle

*featuring* TAGARIS SYRAH

**1½ Tbsp whole coriander seeds**

**4 Tbsp olive oil**

**5 medium shallots, sliced**

**¼ bunch fresh thyme**

**½ cup brown sugar**

**1 bottle Cabernet vinegar (7 oz)**

**1 bottle Syrah**
   **4 king salmon fillets (7 oz each, block cut)**

**1 bunch fresh cilantro, chopped**

**1 bunch fresh basil, chopped**

**1 bunch fresh parsley, chopped**

**1 bunch green onions, chopped**

**salt and freshly ground black pepper to taste**

*This is one of the many fine dishes you're likely to find if you visit The Taverna at Tagaris. Chef Chris Ainsworth uses the finest ingredients of the Pacific Northwest to create mouth-watering Mediterranean-inspired dishes. Syrah is one of 16 varieties of wine grapes grown on the north and south sides of Saddle Mountain near the Wahluke Slope. King salmon are more commonly known as chinook salmon.*

*1.* Toast the coriander seeds in a dry saucepan over medium-high heat for about 2 minutes.

*2.* Add 2 Tbsp of the olive oil and sweat the shallots over medium high heat for about 2 minutes. Add the thyme and brown sugar and cook until the sugar has melted. Add the vinegar and cook until reduced by ⅔. Add the Syrah and cook until reduced by ¾. Strain (the reduction should be a smooth syrupy consistency). Set it aside to cool.

*3.* Coat the salmon with the herbs and green onions. Heat the remaining 2 Tbsp olive oil in a cast iron frying pan over high heat until it's just starting to smoke. Season the salmon with salt and pepper and sear it until it's golden brown, about 3–4 minutes on each side.

*4.* The hot seared salmon is delicious served on a bed of greens dressed with a light vinaigrette. Drizzle a little reduction over the salmon and some around the plate.

SERVES 4

**TAGARIS WINERY**
844 Tulip Lane, Richland
TEL: (509) 628-0020
www.tagariswines.com
info@tagariswines.com

WINE SHOP, TOURS AND TASTINGS
Open for wine tasting, but please call
ahead for details. The patio is open
all day in the summer months for
light dining.

GETTING THERE
From Seattle head east on I-82 to
exit 102, interchange for I-182. Head
east on I-182 to exit 3, Queensgate
Road. Turn right on Queensgate to
Columbia Park Trail. Turn left on
Columbia Park Trail, and then make
an immediate left onto Windmill
Road. Turn right onto Tulip Lane.

WINERY HIGHLIGHTS
Check the website to find out more
about live musicians playing at the
winery and The Taverna.

# Pepper Bridge Porcini-Crusted Sea Bass with White Truffle Aïoli

*featuring* PEPPER BRIDGE WINERY MERLOT

1 egg yolk

1 Tbsp water

1 cup pomace olive oil

5 Tbsp lemon juice

pinch kosher salt

2 tsp white truffle cream

6 sea bass fillets (3 oz each)

salt and freshly ground black
    pepper to taste

3 Tbsp dried porcini
    mushrooms, crushed

2 Tbsp finely diced shallots

1 Tbsp minced fresh thyme

2 Tbsp minced fresh chives

2 Tbsp extra virgin olive oil

¼ cup white wine

¼ cup butter

1 pinch freshly ground black
    pepper

10 oz fresh capellini pasta

*Chef Bear of the famous Marcus Whitman Hotel has come up with this excellent recipe designed to pair with the Pepper Bridge Merlot. This is one of the few recipes in this book where the wine used as an ingredient is not the one suggested for consuming with the meal. Pepper Bridge Merlot is rich, concentrated and plush, and it finishes with a smooth, refined elegance.*

1. Combine the egg yolk and water in a blender. Drizzle in the pomace olive oil while the blender is running (this can also be done by hand, whisking vigorously as you drizzle in the olive oil). Scrape down the sides of the blender and add 4 Tbsp of the lemon juice, salt and white truffle cream. Process briefly and adjust the seasonings if necessary. Set the aïoli aside.

2. Pat the fillets dry with a paper towel. Season each side lightly with salt and pepper, porcini mushrooms, shallots and herbs.

3. Heat the oil in a large sauté pan over medium-high heat until it shimmers. Add the fish and sear each side for about 2 minutes, being careful not to overcook it. Remove the fish from the pan and set aside. Deglaze the pan by adding the wine, 1 Tbsp lemon juice and butter. Cook and stir over the heat, scraping any bits from the bottom of the pan. When the butter has fully melted and become infused with the wine, set the pan aside.

**PEPPER BRIDGE WINERY**
1704 JB George Road, Walla Walla
TEL: (509) 525-6502
FAX: (509) 525-9227
www.pepperbridge.com
info@pepperbridge.com

WINE SHOP, TOURS AND TASTINGS
Open daily 10 a.m.–4 p.m. A small
tasting fee is refunded on purchase.

GETTING THERE
From Washington Highway 125 head
east on Stateline Road then north
on Peppers Road. Then go east on
JB George for about 1 mile before
turning north at the winery sign,
where the road takes a hard right.

WINERY HIGHLIGHTS
Bring a picnic to enjoy on the deck.
There are spectacular views of the
vineyard and the Blue Mountains.

4. Drop the pasta into a large pot of lightly salted boiling water and cook for 1–2 minutes, then drain. Twist some pasta on a fork to form a nice tight roll and place in the center of each plate. Place a fish fillet on top and spoon some pan sauce overtop the fish and pasta. Just off to the side add a dollop of the white truffle aïoli.

5. Serve with Pepper Bridge Merlot.

SERVES 6

# Poultry

I went on a diet, swore off drinking and
heavy eating and in 14 days I lost two weeks.

—*Joe E. Lewis*

# Arbor Crest's Chicken Fiesta!

*featuring* ARBOR CREST RIESLING

3 Tbsp butter

1 green bell pepper, chopped

1 large yellow onion, chopped

2 cloves garlic, minced

2 Tbsp all-purpose flour

⅓ cup Riesling

1 jar salsa (7 oz)

1 can chopped tomatoes,
   including juice (15 oz)

1 can stewed tomatoes, drained
   (15 oz)

1 cup sour cream

salt and freshly ground black
   pepper to taste

1 large bag tortilla chips

3-4 cups cooked and diced
   chicken breast

½ lb cheddar cheese, grated
   (use more if you want)

1 small can chili peppers, diced
   (4 oz, optional)

*This simple but delightful dish also makes a great starter. The best part is the whole thing can be prepared well ahead of time and reheated as necessary. The Arbor Crest Riesling is from the noble white Riesling grape grown in the Columbia Valley. All the grapes are hand-picked and hand-sorted. Slightly sweet, with flavors of pineapple, lemon and honey, this is a great aperitif wine and is also very food friendly.*

*1.* Preheat the oven to 350°F. Heat the butter in a large frying pan over medium-high heat. Sauté the green pepper, onion and garlic for 5–6 minutes and then sprinkle with the flour. Stir and cook for 1 minute. Add the wine, salsa and tomatoes. Bring to a boil, then simmer for 5 minutes. Stir in the sour cream. Remove the pan from the heat. Season with salt and pepper.

*2.* Place a layer of sauce in the bottom of a 4- to 6-quart casserole dish. Add a layer of tortilla chips, then chicken, then cheese. Repeat 2 or 3 times, depending on the depth of the casserole dish, ending with the sauce. Top with the chilies if you are using them. Once the dish is assembled, it can be covered and refrigerated until needed.

*3.* Bake uncovered for 45–60 minutes before serving. Enjoy it with a glass of Arbor Crest Riesling.

SERVES 4

## ARBOR CREST WINE CELLARS

4705 North Fruithill Road, Spokane

TEL: (509) 927-9463

www.arborcrest.com

shelby@arborcrest.com

### WINE SHOP, TOURS AND TASTINGS

Tasting room open daily noon–5 p.m.

### GETTING THERE

Take I-90 (east from Spokane, west from Coeur d'Alene) to Argonne exit 287. Travel north on Argonne and cross the Spokane River. Turn right on Upriver Drive; proceed 1 mile and as the road forks, bear left onto Fruithill Road. Make a sharp right turn at the top of the hill. You are now on Arbor Crest's driveway.

### WINERY HIGHLIGHTS

The winery is located in a 3-storey Florentine house surrounded by an arched gatekeeper's house, sunken rose garden, open air pagoda, terraced flower and herb gardens and a life-sized checkerboard.

# Riesling

*pronounced* (Reez-ling)

*The Riesling grape has its origins in the Rhine and Mosel river valleys in Germany. This grape can thrive in cool climates and is very resistant to frosts. The grape is also known as Johannesburg Riesling, Rhine Riesling or White Riesling. Rieslings can differ in style and can be made into sweet or dry wines, although a semi-dry wine is probably the most common.*

*There are huge plantings of Riesling in Washington, where the grape has been grown since the mid-1800s. While many regions in the world are pulling up their Riesling vines to concentrate on other varietals, here the grape remains strong. This says a lot about the quality of the Washington Rieslings.*

*Riesling is notoriously late to ripen and it is usually the last crop of the year to be harvested. It often frustrates growers as they impatiently wait for the grapes to reach the desired sugar levels.*

*Washington Rieslings usually have perfumey aromas and fresh fruit flavors. Riesling is well suited to many types of food; it goes well with fish and seafood as well as Mexican and Asian foods. Even sushi or curry can be paired with this versatile wine.*

# Wine-Roasted Chicken

1 Tbsp dried oregano

1 Tbsp dried basil

1 Tbsp dried thyme

1 Tbsp paprika

½ cup butter

1 large chicken (5-6 lb)

2 large onions, quartered

5 cloves garlic, halved

3 cups chicken stock

1 cup white wine

salt and black freshly ground
    pepper to taste

*There is no food more homely than roast chicken. That wonderful aroma really fills up the house on a Sunday afternoon. We always try to buy free-range birds; we honestly believe they taste better.*

1. Preheat the oven to 375°F. In a small bowl combine the dried herbs and paprika with the butter. Rinse the chicken well under running water and pat dry with paper towel.

2. Carefully lift the chicken skin and rub the herb butter between the skin and the breast. Get as far in as you can without damaging the skin. Butter the outside of the skin as well. Every part of the chicken should be buttered. Insert 4 of the onion quarters in the bird's cavity. Use a skewer or string to truss the legs together. Put the chicken in a roasting pan with the remaining 4 onion wedges and the garlic cloves. Pour the chicken stock and wine directly over the chicken.

3. Bake in the oven for about 2½ hours for a 6-lb bird. Add or subtract about 20 minutes for each lb more or less. It's important to baste the bird with the pan juices every 30 minutes. For the last 15 minutes of cooking crank up the oven to 425°F to get the skin crispy.

4. Remove the chicken from the pan and tent loosely with foil. Use a spoon or fork to crush up the garlic cloves in the bottom of the pan and stir well to make the gravy. It may seem unusual, but it's tastier than gravy thickened with flour. Let the bird rest for about 30 minutes before carving. Reheat the pan juices just before serving.

SERVES 6

# Chicken with Plums and Figs

*featuring* CHARDONNAY

*Here is another great recipe that comes from the kitchen at Arbor Crest Winery. The combination of chicken and fruit is heavenly and the Arbor Crest Chardonnay complements both.*

1½ cups Chardonnay

3 Tbsp tomato paste

3 Tbsp minced garlic

3 Tbsp brown sugar

1½ tsp dried oregano

1½ tsp kosher salt

1½ tsp poultry seasoning

1½ tsp chicken stock powder

1½ cups marinated artichoke hearts, drained

1 cup pitted dried plums

1 cup dried figs, halved

3 Tbsp capers, rinsed and drained

2 lb boneless chicken breasts

2 Tbsp sour cream

1. Combine the wine, tomato paste, garlic, brown sugar, oregano, salt, poultry seasoning and chicken stock powder in a bowl and mix well. Stir in the artichoke hearts, plums, figs and capers.

2. Arrange the chicken in a single layer in a baking dish. Spoon the wine mixture over the chicken, turning to coat. Cover and marinate in the refrigerator for 2–10 hours, turning occasionally.

3. Preheat the oven to 350°F. Bake the chicken for 1 hour. Remove the chicken pieces to a serving platter with a slotted spoon. Stir the sour cream into the sauce and pour over the chicken. Serve immediately with basmati rice, couscous or mashed potato.

SERVES 4

# Ash Hollow Duck Legs Braised in Red Wine with Blackberries

*featuring* ASH HOLLOW CABERNET SAUVIGNON

4 duck legs

1 cup Cabernet Sauvignon

10 cloves garlic, crushed

10 sprigs fresh thyme

6 shallots, peeled

2 cups fresh blackberries

4 cups duck stock (or chicken stock)

salt and freshly ground black pepper to taste

*Duck is great with fruit, and although duck à l'orange may be more famous, this recipe tastes better. The dark garnet color foretells the richness of this wine, with classic notes of cedar and red currants along with a touch of white sage. The wine has a firm acidity, balanced by fruit notes and supple tannins with a long, lingering finish, making it a great pairing for this recipe.*

*1.* Season the duck legs on both sides with salt and pepper. Sear the duck in a heavy ovenproof pan over medium-high heat until browned on both sides, about 10 minutes in total. The skin should be crisp. (Do not add fat to the pan; the duck skin will render enough fat to keep it from sticking.) If you like, you can save the fat left in the pan for delicious roast potatoes or a duck confit.

*2.* Preheat the oven to 350°F. After draining off the fat, add the wine to deglaze the pan and scrape up all the brown bits. Add the garlic, thyme and shallots and cook over high heat until the liquid is reduced by half. Add half the blackberries and then the duck legs. Add just enough stock to cover the duck legs.

*3.* Place in the oven uncovered and cook for 1½ –2 hours. The duck meat should be so tender it falls off the bones. Pour the braising liquid into a saucepan over medium-high heat. Skim off any fat. Add the rest of the blackberries and season with salt and pepper. Let the sauce simmer until slightly thickened, about 5–10 minutes.

*4.* Serve with rosemary and garlic roasted potatoes or mushroom risotto. Pour yourself a glass of Ash Hollow Cabernet Sauvignon. *Bon appetit!*

SERVES 4

## ASH HOLLOW WINERY

14 North 2nd Avenue, Walla Walla

TEL: (509) 529-7565

FAX: (509) 529-2365

www.ashhollow.com

heidi@ashhollow.com

### WINE SHOP, TOURS AND TASTINGS

Summer hours: Wed.–Sat. noon–
8 p.m. and Sun. noon–4 p.m. But
the "real" hours are "if the doors are
open, then they are open!"

### GETTING THERE

Just off Main Street in Walla Walla.

### WINERY HIGHLIGHTS

The work of local artists is featured
in the tasting room. The tasting
room is located in the Dice Building,
named after A.K. Dice, who used the
building for his dentistry practice
and was the first licensed dentist
in Washington State. You can also
arrange a customized wine tour
with Blue Stocking Tours (www.
bluestockingtours.com
(509) 522-4717).

# Cabernet Sauvignon

*pronounced (CA-BURR-NAY SOH-VIN-YON)*

*Cabernet Sauvignon, or Cab Sav as it is affectionately termed by some wine lovers, is one of the most popular red wines in the world. The grape can be traced back to the Médoc district in the Bordeaux region of France, where it is still prominent today.*

*The grapes often ripen mid- to late-season, and conditions in Washington are generally regarded as even better for growing than those in France or California. In fact, many believe that Washington produces the world's best Cabernet Sauvignon.*

*Cabernet Sauvignon is fantastic for aging, and good wines very often become great wines after cellaring. Cabernet Sauvignon also blends remarkably well, and when combined with Merlot it becomes a little mellower without losing its character.*

*Pair Cabernet Sauvignon with steak, pasta with tomato based sauces, dark meats, duck, blue cheese and dark chocolate. Known to many as "The King of Red Wine," this variety is unlikely to lose its crown any time soon.*

# Boudreaux Cellars Delicious Saffron Quail

*featuring* BOUDREAUX CHARDONNAY FROM BISHOP'S AND HOMESTEAD VINEYARDS

4 quails

salt and freshly ground black
    pepper to taste

3 Tbsp olive oil

8 cloves garlic, chopped

1 large carrot, peeled and
    sliced into thin rounds

2 bunches green onions, cut in
    1-inch lengths

½ cup Chardonnay

¼ cup butter

1½ tsp dried rosemary

2 pinches saffron

12 oz angel hair pasta (cooked
    as instructed on packet)

*This wine was barrel-fermented through complete malolactic (secondary) fermentation in French and Minnesota barrels. It is unfiltered, cold stabilized and bottled in heavy Burgundian glass with the highest quality cork. Winemaker and owner Rob Newsom came up with this delicious recipe, which is great for special occasions or just for treating yourself.*

*1.* Preheat the oven to 400°F. Generously salt and pepper the quails. Heat the olive oil in a large cast iron frying pan over medium-high heat and brown the quails for 3–4 minutes. Add the garlic, carrot, green onions and wine. Sauté for another 2 minutes. Stir in the butter and rosemary and remove from the heat.

*2.* Pour all the ingredients into a presoaked clay baking dish (or any covered baking dish). Sprinkle in the saffron and bake covered for about 1 hour. After 30 minutes, stir to ensure the quails are moist. The exact cooking time will depend on the size of the quails, so check that they are cooked through. The juice will reduce during cooking.

*3.* Swish the angel hair pasta in the frying pan used to brown the quails. Place on serving plates and top with the quails and the juice. Serve with a wild green salad with plenty of arugula. Enjoy a glass of Boudreaux Chardonnay or the Boudreaux Merlot.

SERVES 4

**BOUDREAUX CELLARS**

4551 Icicle Creek Road, Leavenworth

TEL: (509) 548-5858

www.boudreauxcellars.com

rob@boudreauxcellars.com

WINE SHOP, TOURS AND TASTINGS

As the winery is also the Newsoms'
home, visits are by appointment only.
Check the website for details on their
barrel tastings.

GETTING THERE

The winery is located just
7½ miles up Icicle Creek Road
from Leavenworth.

WINERY HIGHLIGHTS

These are small lots of handcrafted,
premium wines with grapes sourced
from the best Washington State
vineyards.

# Maryhill's Mouth-Watering Roast Game Hens

*featuring* MARYHILL PROPRIETOR'S RESERVE ZINFANDEL

4 Cornish game hens

2 Tbsp Chinese five-spice
    powder

1 Tbsp salt

2 cups sliced fresh peaches

2 cups sliced fresh apples

½ cup raisins

½ cup diced onion

2 cups Zinfandel

¼ cup sugar

dash ground cinnamon

*In this fine Zinfandel, winemaker John Haw has coalesced bold
jam and cooked plum flavors with a pleasing oak background.
John's signature late-harvest style allows the wine to retain
much of its original grape sugars. Aromas of freshly popped
walnut shells and eucalyptus exude from this wine, 100 percent
aged in new French oak barrels. The fruity flavors of the wine
mix wonderfully with the fruit in the recipe to create bold,
mouth-watering flavors in the sauce.*

1.  Split the game hens in half with a sharp knife. Rinse the
    halves and pat them dry, then rub five-spice powder and
    salt all over them. Preheat the oven to 375°F.

2.  Stew the peaches, apples, raisins, onions, Zinfandel,
    sugar and cinnamon in a medium-sized pan over
    medium-high heat until it begins to reduce to a syrup
    with fruity chunks.

3.  Transfer the fruit mixture to a baking dish and place the
    hens on top of the mixture. Bake for 40 minutes.

4.  Serve with mashed potatoes, fresh asparagus and a glass of
    Maryhill Proprietor's Reserve Zinfandel.

SERVES 4–6

## MARYHILL WINERY

9774 Highway 14, Goldendale
TEL: (509) 773-1976 or
1 (877) 627-9445
TEL: (509) 773-0586
www.maryhillwinery.com
vickil@maryhillwinery.com

### WINE SHOP, TOURS AND TASTINGS

Open daily 10 a.m.–6 p.m. with an
extensive gift shop and self-service
deli. Free wine tasting. Reserve
flights for a fee. Two tours every Sat.
and Sun.

### GETTING THERE

From Seattle take I-90 east to
Ellensburg and then I-82 to Yakima.
Just past Yakima take the 97 south to
Goldendale. Just before the river take
Route 14 west to the winery, which is
just past the Maryhill museum.

### WINERY HIGHLIGHTS

Beautiful views of Mount Hood and
the Columbia River Gorge. There
is a 4,000-seat amphitheater for
summer concerts and picnicking.

### CHEF'S TIP

*Although Chinese five-spice powder is readily available at supermarkets and Asian grocery stores, it can also be fun to make your own. Just roast 2 tsp of Szechuan (or black) peppercorns in a dry pan over low heat for 2–3 minutes. Grind the peppercorns and combine with 4 tsp ground anise, ½ tsp ground cloves, 1 Tbsp ground cinnamon and 1 Tbsp ground fennel. Mix well and grind the entire mix again if desired.*

# Chicken Parmigiana

3 Tbsp olive oil

½ onion, diced

3 cloves garlic, crushed

salt and freshly ground black pepper to taste

1 can chopped tomatoes (28 oz)

¾ cup red wine

1 tsp sugar

4 large chicken breast halves (boneless)

1 Tbsp seasoning salt

½ cup all-purpose flour

2 eggs, beaten

1½ cups dry breadcrumbs

¾ cup grated mozzarella cheese

½ cup grated Parmesan cheese

*This dish takes its name from the Italian city of Parma. Originally, 400 years ago, this dish was made with veal and there were no tomatoes or cheese in it at all. The recipe has evolved since then and now tomatoes and cheese play an important part. We have used red wine to create the rich tomato sauce, which is delicious over the juicy chicken breasts.*

1. Heat 1 Tbsp of the olive oil in a large pan over medium heat. Add the onion and sauté for about 5 minutes, stirring frequently. Add the garlic and lightly season with salt and pepper. Continue to sauté for another 2 minutes.

2. Add the tomatoes and their juice and increase the heat to high. Stir frequently for about 10 minutes, until the excess liquid has mostly evaporated. Reduce the heat to medium high, then add the wine and sugar. Cook for about 15–20 minutes longer until the liquid has evaporated. Put half the tomato mixture in a blender or food processor and blend until smooth. Mix with the unblended tomato mixture and set aside.

3. Cover the chicken with plastic wrap or wax paper. Using the flat side of a meat mallet or a rolling pin, gently pound the chicken breasts and flatten them out to about ¼ inch. Season them with the seasoning salt and dust them with flour. Dip them into the beaten egg and then the breadcrumbs. Press firmly to ensure the crumbs adhere.

4. Heat the remaining 2 Tbsp oil over medium-high heat in a large frying pan and cook the chicken for about 3 minutes on each side, until golden brown and almost cooked through. Transfer the chicken to a baking dish and cover with the tomato sauce (you may have leftover sauce, which will keep for up to a week and is great for pizzas or toasted cheese sandwiches!).

5. Combine the mozzarella and Parmesan cheeses. Top the chicken with the cheese mixture and place under the broiler, about 4 inches from the heat source, for 5–8 minutes or until the cheese is golden brown and the chicken is cooked through.

SERVES 4

# Masset Winery Braised Duck

*featuring* MASSET WINERY RESERVE SYRAH

8 duck hindquarters (leg and thigh, bone in)

2 cups all-purpose flour

3 Tbsp kosher salt

2 tsp white pepper

¼ cup grapeseed oil (can substitute olive oil if necessary)

1 medium onion, chopped

16 cloves garlic, peeled

1 cup Syrah

1 quart rich duck stock (or beef stock)

2 sprigs fresh thyme

1 small sprig fresh rosemary

*Executive Chef Greg Masset of the Yakima Country Club is also a winemaker and he creates marvelous dishes to go with his fabulous wines. This is his tasty, simple recipe for braised duck. Masset Winery Reserve Syrah is a popular wine, so if you're able to get your hands on some, this dish is an appropriate way to celebrate your good luck.*

*1.* Preheat the oven to 325°F. Pat the duck dry with a paper towel. Reserve 3 Tbsp of the flour and mix the rest with the salt and pepper. Dredge the duck in the flour mixture.

*2.* Heat the oil in a large frying pan over medium-high heat. Quickly brown the meat, about 2 minutes on each side, then remove to a casserole dish. Add the onion and garlic to the pan and sauté for 2 minutes. Stir in the remaining 3 Tbsp of flour. Add the wine and continue cooking to reduce. When the pan is almost dry, add the stock and fresh herbs and bring to a boil. Pour the mixture over the duck.

*3.* Cover the dish with foil and bake for 1½–2 hours, until fork tender. Serve the duck with roasted fingerling potatoes, asparagus and Masset Winery Reserve Syrah.

SERVES 4

MASSET WINERY
620 East Parker Heights Road
Wapato
TEL: (509) 877-6675
www.massetwinery.com
massetwine@nwinfo.com

WINE SHOP, TOURS AND TASTINGS
Complimentary tastings Feb.–Nov.,
Thu.–Sun. Call to confirm hours.

GETTING THERE
Head north at exit 44 off I-82. Turn
left at Yakima Valley Highway and
right onto East Parker Heights Road.
Stay right and the winery is ⅔ mile
ahead on the right.

WINERY HIGHLIGHTS
The tasting room is housed in
the historic 1905 Angel family
farmhouse. The gift shop features
gourmet items, candles and select
bath products.

# Meat

Wine is the intellectual part of a meal,
meats are merely the material part.

—*Alexandre Dumas Sr.*

# Arbutus Beef Wellington

*featuring* Arbutus Winery Cabernet Sauvignon

1 beef tenderloin, fat trimmed
   (3–4 lb)

2 Tbsp olive oil

salt and freshly ground black
   pepper to taste

2 Tbsp butter

¾ lb crimini mushrooms, finely
   chopped

2 Tbsp chopped shallots

¼ cup Cabernet Sauvignon

1 package puff pastry, thawed

1 large egg yolk

*This recipe has been adapted by Arbutus from one that appeared in* Sunset *magazine. It takes some time to prepare but it's worth it, and a lot of steps can be done in advance. This Cabernet Sauvignon is a rich, full-bodied wine that can be enjoyed alone or paired with meat, spicy foods or chocolate. This dish is even better when served with Cabernet Béarnaise Sauce, page 151.*

*1.* Preheat the oven to 400°F. Rinse the tenderloin and pat it dry, then rub it with olive oil, salt and pepper. Place the tenderloin on a rack in a shallow pan. Roast for about 30 minutes or until the thickest part reads 120°F on a meat thermometer. Cover and chill until cool, about 4 hours. Skim the fat from the pan juices. (If you want to make the béarnaise sauce, reserve the drippings, mix with ¼ cup water and refrigerate; otherwise discard.)

*2.* Melt the butter in a heavy frying pan over medium-high heat. Sauté the mushrooms and shallots for about 2 minutes. Add the wine, stirring frequently until the liquid evaporates, about 6–8 minutes. Set the mushroom mixture aside to cool.

*3.* Unfold the puff pastry on a floured surface and roll out into a rectangle large enough to enclose the tenderloin completely. Distribute the cooled mushroom mixture over the pastry, spreading it to within 1 inch of the edge. Place the tenderloin lengthwise in the center of the mushroom mixture and enclose it in the pastry, tucking in the ends of the pastry to completely cover the meat.

ARBUTUS WINERY
West Seattle
TEL: (206) 498-3348
www.arbutuswinery.com
arbutus@arbutuswinery.com

WINE SHOP, TOURS AND TASTINGS
The winery is not presently open to
the public. Check the website for
updated details.

WINERY HIGHLIGHTS
Arbutus Winery, a small winery
located in scenic West Seattle,
makes rich, full-bodied red wines
using grapes harvested from top
Washington vineyards. All wines
are handcrafted in limited quantities
and are available from the winery by
contacting them directly.

**4.** Beat the egg yolk in a small bowl with 1 Tbsp of
water. Brush the egg mixture over the pastry. Place
the tenderloin seam side down on an oiled pan.

**5.** Preheat the oven to 400°F. Bake until the pastry is
golden brown, about 20 minutes. Reduce the heat
to 350°F and continue baking for 10 minutes, until
the meat reaches 140°F for medium rare. Transfer to
a serving platter and let rest for at least 10 minutes
before slicing. This dish should be enjoyed with a glass
of Arbutus Cabernet Sauvignon.

SERVES 8—10

# Barrister's Tenderloin of Beef with Merlot Sauce

*featuring* BARRISTER WINERY RED MOUNTAIN MERLOT

1 whole tenderloin (4–5 lb), fat
   and silver skin removed

½ cup clarified butter

3 oz cognac

2½ Tbsp butter

1 shallot, chopped

½ cup Merlot

1¼ cups beef stock

1 Tbsp cornstarch, dissolved in
   ¼ cup Merlot, stock or
   water

⅓ cup tomato sauce

salt and freshly ground black
   pepper to taste

*This award-winning Merlot is from the outstanding Artz Vineyard on Red Mountain, Washington State's smallest appellation. While not a wine for the timid, the Merlot has soft tannins so you can enjoy it in its youth or in a couple of years as it matures. We suggest you decant this wine so it can open up to reveal its true breadth of aroma and flavors. Search the local farmers' markets for particularly attractive fresh garden vegetables to serve with this classic dish.*

*1.* Preheat the oven to 350°F. Coat the beef with the clarified butter, place in an ovenproof frying pan and bake in the oven for around 45 minutes or until the meat reaches the desired doneness. A meat thermometer should read 140°F for medium rare.

*2.* Remove the beef from the oven and cover with the cognac. Light the cognac and when the flame goes out, place the tenderloin on a serving platter and cover with foil to keep warm. Set the frying pan and juices aside.

*3.* In a separate pan melt 1½ Tbsp of the butter over medium-high heat and sauté the shallots for 3–4 minutes. Add the wine and let the liquid reduce by ¾. Add 1 cup of the beef stock and bring to a boil before stirring in the dissolved cornstarch, tomato sauce, salt and pepper.

4. Place the roasting frying pan on the stovetop over medium heat. Add the remaining ¼ cup of beef stock and scrape the bottom of the pan with a wooden spoon to dislodge any browned bits. Add the Merlot sauce and simmer before adding the remaining 1 Tbsp of butter.

5. Pour a little of the Merlot sauce directly over the roast and serve the remaining sauce separately.

SERVES 8–10

# Chateau Ste. Michelle's Boneless Leg of Lamb

*featuring* CHATEAU STE. MICHELLE INDIAN WELLS MERLOT

¾ cup **Merlot**

½ cup olive oil

1 Tbsp Dijon mustard

2 Tbsp chopped fresh
rosemary

2 Tbsp chopped Italian parsley

4 cloves garlic, chopped

salt and coarse black pepper
to taste

1 lamb leg (have the butcher
bone it and fillet it open)

*This is a lush and fleshy New World–style Merlot loaded with the jammy blackberry flavors characteristic of warm climate Wahluke Slope fruit. Here the wine is paired with a fabulous and simple lamb recipe by John Sarich, the Culinary Director of the winery.*

1. Combine all the ingredients except the lamb. Rub the mixture over the entire lamb leg and let it stand for 2 hours, turning and rubbing it occasionally.

2. Preheat the grill to medium-high or the oven to 350°F. This dish is best grilled over charcoal, but will do fine cooked in the oven. For rare meat, cook until a meat thermometer registers 140°F.

3. To serve, cut thinly across the grain and fan out on a plate. Enjoy with a glass of Chateau Ste. Michelle Indian Wells Merlot.

SERVES 4–6

## CHATEAU STE. MICHELLE
14111 NE 145th Street, Woodinville
TEL: (425) 415-3300
FAX: (425) 415-3657
www.chateau-ste-michelle.com
info@ste-michelle.com

WINE SHOP, TOURS AND TASTINGS
Complimentary tours and tastings
offered daily 10 a.m.–4:30 p.m.
Gift and retail wine shop open daily
10 a.m.–5 p.m. Reserve, single-
vineyard and library wines are
available in the winery's Vintage
Reserve Room for an $8 sampling
fee. Call (425) 415-3633 to book
an appointment.

GETTING THERE
From I-405 take exit 23 heading east.
Get in the right lane and take the first
exit for Highway 202 East. Go down
the hill and under the train trestle
to the stoplight at NE 175th Street.
Turn right and cross over the railroad
tracks and continue to the 4-way
stop. Turn left and take Highway
202 for approximately 2 miles to
the winery.

WINERY HIGHLIGHTS
Chateau Ste. Michelle was named
2005 Winery of the Year by
*Restaurant Wine* and 2004
American Winery of the Year by
*Wine Enthusiast. Wine and Spirits*
magazine has named it Winery of
the Year an incredible 10 times!

# Forgeron Cellars Grilled Hanger Steak with Crispy Onions

*featuring* FORGERON CABERNET SAUVIGNON

½ cup green peppercorns

1 bottle Cabernet Sauvignon

1½ cups extra virgin olive oil

1 Tbsp chopped garlic

3 bay leaves

1 Tbsp chopped thyme leaves

1 lb hanger steak

1 cup sugar

1 lb butter at room temperature

salt and freshly ground black pepper to taste

½ cup cornstarch

½ cup all-purpose flour

1 yellow onion, sliced into thin rings

*Chef Michael Riley, Executive Chef of the Courtyard Marriott in Richland, came up with this dish to highlight the Forgeron Cabernet Sauvignon. The recipe calls for a lot of wine, but you are left with extra Cabernet Sauvignon butter, which can be frozen or stored in the refrigerator and used in many other recipes. The wine is luscious and satisfying from start to finish, showing the fine art of blending many flavors from different terroirs to achieve complexity and depth. Well-rounded tannins and a nice acidity contribute to a long finish. This is a wine that has great potential for cellaring.*

*1.* Most of the preparation needs to be done the day before serving the meal. In a blender or food processor combine 1 Tbsp of the green peppercorns, ½ cup of the wine, ½ cup of the olive oil and the garlic, bay leaves and thyme. Blend until smooth. Place the steaks in a non-metallic container, pour the sauce overtop, cover and refrigerate overnight.

*2.* To make the Cabernet Sauvignon butter, combine the remaining wine with the sugar in a saucepan and bring to a boil. Reduce the heat to low and simmer until it is the consistency of syrup, about 30 minutes. Allow the syrup to cool. Combine the syrup and butter in a bowl and mix thoroughly. Season with salt and pepper. Roll into logs, enclose in plastic wrap and store in the refrigerator.

*3.* To make the green peppercorn oil process the remaining 1 cup of olive oil with the remaining green peppercorns in a blender. Store in a jar or bottle at room temperature.

FORGERON CELLARS

33 West Birch Street, Walla Walla

TEL: (509) 522-9463

FAX: (509) 522-0037

www.forgeroncellars.com

info@forgeroncellars.com

WINE SHOP, TOURS AND TASTINGS
Open for free tastings daily 11 a.m.–
4 p.m. Tours are available by
appointment only.

GETTING THERE
 From State Highway 12, take the
2nd Avenue/City Center exit. Turn
south onto 2nd Avenue and continue
approximately 9 blocks to Birch
Street. Turn right onto Birch, go
1 block and the winery is located
on the southeast corner.

WINERY HIGHLIGHTS
The tasting room is a renovated turn-
of-the-century blacksmith shop. Be
sure to say hello to Salsa, the official
greeter. You'll recognize her by her
black coat and wet nose.

**4.** Make the onions on the day of the meal. Combine the cornstarch, flour, salt and pepper and dredge the sliced onions in the mixture. Deep fry at 375°F for about 1 minute, or until crispy.

**5.** Finally, grill the marinated hanger steaks to your desired doneness (about 4 minutes on each side for medium rare). Slice the steak thinly against the grain and serve on a mound of creamed potatoes. Top with pats of Cabernet Sauvignon butter and some crispy onions. Drizzle with the green peppercorn oil. Open another bottle of Forgeron Cabernet Sauvignon and enjoy!

SERVES 2

# Fort Walla Walla Cellars Sweet and Sour Pork Ribs

*featuring* FORT WALLA WALLA CELLARS SYRAH

**4 lb country-style boneless pork spare ribs**

**granulated garlic and freshly ground black pepper to taste**

**1½ cups Syrah**

**36 oz honey-based BBQ sauce**

**½ cup brown sugar**

**1 can pineapple chunks (6 oz, drained)**

**1 large onion, sliced in strips**

**1 green pepper, sliced in strips**

*Chocolate lovers will enjoy Fort Walla Walla Cellars Syrah from the first whiff as it is loaded with dark Godiva aromas backed with dusty cherry notes. It is a full-bodied wine with flavors of blackberries and sweet chocolate and slightly earthy overtones—a delicious Rhône-style Syrah that stands up beautifully to these tasty ribs!*

1. Preheat the oven to 375°F. Rub the ribs with granulated garlic and pepper to taste. Bake for 45 minutes. Drain the grease and liquid from the ribs.

2. Mix the remaining ingredients well in a large bowl and pour over the drained ribs. Continue to bake for another 40 minutes.

3. Serve over hot rice and enjoy with a bottle of Fort Walla Cellars Syrah.

SERVES 6

FORT WALLA WALLA CELLARS

1383 Barleen Drive, Walla Walla
(see tasting room address below)
TEL: (509) 520-1095
FAX: (509) 529-7808
www.fortwallawallacellars.com
info@fortwallawallacellars.com

WINE SHOP, TOURS AND TASTINGS

Fort Walla Walla Cellars Tasting
Room is located at 127 East Main
Street. Open Thu.–Mon. 10 a.m.–
4:30 p.m. No charge for tasting.

GETTING THERE

Downtown Walla Walla on the corner
of Main and Spokane streets.

WINERY HIGHLIGHTS

This is a small boutique winery that
annually produces about 1,600 cases
of exceptional Bordeaux- and Rhône-
style wines from grapes grown in the
Walla Walla Valley.

# Syrah

*pronounced* (SEE-RAHH)

*This grape, known as Shiraz in South Africa and Australia, has a long history. Many romantic historians believe it was originally grown in southern Iran, near the village of Shiraz, and was taken back to France by the crusaders some time between the 11th and 13th centuries. Others contend the grape has always been a native of France.*

*In France, the grape was originally grown in the Rhone Valley, where it was developed into the style of wine we have come to love. Washington now has thousands of acres of these vines and is becoming renowned throughout the world for its high-quality Syrah. Many see Washington Syrah overtaking both Cabernet Sauvignon and Merlot in popularity.*

*This variety buds rather late but ripens mid-season. The grape is thick skinned and very dark. The wine is usually deep violet in color and often has aromas and flavors of blackberry, pepper, herbs and cinnamon. When the weather has been warm the wine is fruitier, and cooler seasons give the wine more spicy aromas.*

*Syrah pairs well with heavy foods, such as lamb, steak, duck and game bird, and it's a guaranteed winner with just about anything that has been barbecued.*

# Glen Fiona's Syrah-Braised Beef

*featuring* GLEN FIONA SYRAH

3 Tbsp olive oil

3½ lb beef stewing meat, cut in
   1-inch cubes

1 large onion, chopped

1 bunch parsley, chopped

4 cloves garlic, chopped

2 bay leaves

¼ tsp ground cloves

¼ tsp ground cinnamon

¼ tsp allspice

1 cup Syrah

2 cups beef stock

2 cans tomatoes (15 oz each)

1 cup Kalamata olives, pitted

4 tsp chopped fresh rosemary
   (or 2 tsp dried)

2 red bell peppers, sliced

salt and freshly ground black
   pepper to taste

*This tasty and unusual recipe pairs perfectly with Syrah. Glen Fiona is the original Syrah producer in Walla Walla. The wine is produced in the style of the northern Rhone and features 10 percent Viognier co-fermented with Walla Walla Syrah. It is cold-macerated for 72 hours before fermentation and aged in French oak.*

1. Heat the oil in a large heavy pan over medium-high heat. Add the beef and brown on all sides. Remove from the pan and set aside. Reduce the heat to medium, add the onion and brown for about 10 minutes. Stir in the parsley, garlic, bay leaves, cloves, cinnamon and allspice.

2. Return the beef to the pan and stir well to coat with the onion and spice mixture. Add the wine and beef stock and bring to a boil. Scrape up any brown bits on the bottom of the pan with a wooden spoon and simmer for 15 minutes.

3. Add the tomatoes with their juice and break them up with the spoon. Mix in the olives and rosemary. Reduce the heat to low and simmer for 1½ hours, stirring occasionally. Add the red peppers and simmer for a further 20 minutes. Season to taste with salt and pepper.

4. Serve with potatoes or polenta and accompany with a glass of Glen Fiona Syrah.

SERVES 6

## GLEN FIONA

1249 Lyday Lane, Walla Walla
TEL: (509) 522-2566
FAX: (509) 522-2568
www.glenfiona.com
syrah@glenfiona.com

### WINE SHOP, TOURS AND TASTINGS

Tasting room is open weekends
11 a.m.–4 p.m. and by appointment.

### GETTING THERE

Located near the state line with
Oregon. Travel south on Plaza Way
for around 2 miles until the asphalt
pavement turns to concrete. Turn
left on Brandon Road and follow for
another 1½ miles to Lyday Lane, then
turn right.

### WINERY HIGHLIGHTS

Founded in 1994 as the seventh
winery in Walla Walla, Glen Fiona is
the original producer of Walla Walla
Syrah. Glen Fiona offers a spectacular
view of the Walla Walla Valley.

# Hightower Cellars Lamb Burgers

*featuring* HIGHTOWER CABERNET SAUVIGNON

1 cup plain yogurt

2 Tbsp minced fresh mint leaves

1 tsp fresh lemon juice

1 large garlic clove, halved lengthwise and one half minced

kosher salt to taste

1½ lb ground lamb

¼ cup Cabernet Sauvignon

⅓ cup minced fresh parsley

⅓ cup finely chopped onion

⅛ tsp ground allspice

kosher salt and freshly ground black pepper to taste

4 round slices crusty bread

3 Tbsp olive oil

3-4 cups mixed greens (a bag of spring mix works well)

*This easy-to-prepare lamb recipe can add something special to your barbecue. Hightower Cabernet Sauvignon is a big wine with deep rich color and flavor. It is decadent and full bodied, with hints of chocolate, cherry and blackberry finishing with soft tannins. The wine is sourced from some of the warmest sites in Washington, Red Mountain and Alder Ridge, which are responsible for the intensity and dark fruit. Grapes from a cooler site, Pepper Bridge Vineyard in Walla Walla, provide high-toned cherry fruit.*

1. Preheat the grill to medium. In a small bowl mix the yogurt, mint, lemon juice, minced garlic and salt.

2. In a separate large bowl mix the lamb, wine, parsley, onion and allspice. Season with salt and pepper. Mix thoroughly and form 4 patties.

3. Grill the lamb burgers until they are halfway done, about 7–8 minutes, then flip. Cook another 7–8 minutes or until cooked to the desired doneness. While the burgers are cooking, brush each slice of bread with 1 Tbsp olive oil. Grill the bread on both sides. When the bread is done, rub it with the reserved ½ clove of garlic.

4. Toss the greens with the remaining olive oil and season with salt. Put the burger on top of the grilled bread, spoon yogurt sauce over the burger and top with the greens.

SERVES 4

### HIGHTOWER CELLARS

19418 East 583 PR NE, Benton City
TEL: (509) 588-2867
www.hightowercellars.com
handsorted@hightowercellars.com

WINE SHOP, TOURS AND TASTINGS
Open by appointment and on event
weekends.

GETTING THERE
From I-82 going east or west, take
Benton City exit 96 and head north.
Take the first right onto Highway
224 (at Park and Ride). Turn left
onto Sunset Road, then follow to the
end and turn left onto East 583 PR
NE. Hightower Cellars is the second
driveway on the right.

WINERY HIGHLIGHTS
Great wine, beautiful view, friendly
people and a very friendly dog!

# Lowden Hills Hamburger Walla Walla

*featuring* LOWDEN HILLS WINERY MERLOT

**2 lb ground beef round**

**½ cup Merlot**

**⅓ cup honey smoke–style barbecue sauce**

**2 Tbsp olive oil**

**¼ cup diced Walla Walla sweet onion**

**salt and freshly ground black pepper to taste**

*This simple burger is a perfect addition to a lazy summer day. Lowden Hills Merlot is made with grapes from its Win Chester Vineyards. This full-bodied Merlot is definitely fruit forward, oozing hints of dark cherry, deep currant and a touch of blackberry, all riding on a kiss of subtly integrated oak.*

1. Spread the ground meat out in a large bowl. Add the wine and barbecue sauce and mix well.

2. Heat the oil in a pan over medium heat. Sauté the onion for 3–4 minutes or until golden. Transfer the sautéed onion to the hamburger meat and mix thoroughly. Season with salt and pepper.

3. Allow the meat to sit for 5–10 minutes and then form it into 6 patties. Cover and refrigerate until you're ready to barbecue.

4. Heat the grill to medium-high. Cook the patties for 5 minutes, flip them and cook for another 3 minutes. Reduce the heat to low and cook for a further 2 minutes. All barbecues cook slightly differently, so adjust the time and heat accordingly. Experts recommend you thoroughly cook hamburger meat. Even when cooked, the center may look slightly pink due to the wine and barbecue sauce. (You could also cook this on the stovetop using similar cooking times.)

5. Serve the burgers with your favorite toppings, such as Walla Walla sweet onions, tomato slices, lettuce and pickles.

SERVES 6

LOWDEN HILLS WINERY
535 NE Spitzenburg Street
College Place
TEL: (509) 527-1040
www.lowdenhillswinery.com
info@lowdenhillswinery.com

WINE SHOP, TOURS AND TASTINGS
Open for public tasting year-round
Sat. 11 a.m.–4 p.m. Mar.–Oct.,
Sat.– Mon. 11 a.m.–4 p.m.

GETTING THERE
From Walla Walla drive west on
Rose Street. At Myra Road go south
1 block. Head west at Spitzenburg
Street for 3 blocks to the red barn
with the white roof.

WINERY HIGHLIGHTS
Established in 2002 by Jim and Sonja
Henderson, the winery is working
to become an estate winery. The
2005 vintage is all estate wine to be
released in 2007.

WINERY SPECIAL OFFER
Show this book and receive a free
wine tasting and a drip-stop with
every purchase.

# Sandhill's Pork Ragu

*featuring* SANDHILL CABERNET SAUVIGNON RED MOUNTAIN

1 Tbsp extra virgin olive oil

1 medium yellow onion, diced

2 cloves garlic, crushed

1 stalk celery, diced

1 head fennel, diced

1 medium carrot, diced

1 lb ground pork (preferably heritage pork)

1 cup Cabernet Sauvignon

1 can diced tomatoes (15 oz)

1 bay leaf

½ tsp chopped fresh oregano

½ tsp chopped fresh tarragon

salt and freshly ground black pepper to taste

*The Sandhill Cabernet Sauvignon Red Mountain that was used to create this recipe (adapted by Sandhill from a recipe in the Fall 2005 edition of* Wine and Spirits *magazine) was the 2001 vintage. An estate-grown blend of 95 percent Cabernet Sauvignon and 5 percent Merlot, the wine was aged in small French oak barrels for 19 months and further aged in the bottle for a year prior to release. It has been awarded almost a dozen gold, silver and bronze medals in regional and national competitions.*

1. Heat the olive oil in a large pan over medium heat and sauté the onion, garlic, celery, fennel and carrot for 5 minutes or until they are soft. Add the pork and cook for about 10 minutes. Drain off the excess grease.

2. Add the red wine and reduce until the liquid is mostly gone. Add the tomatoes and bay leaf, cover and simmer for 60 minutes.

3. Skim off any surface fat, then add the oregano and tarragon. Simmer for an additional 30 minutes. Season with salt and pepper.

4. Serve over linguini or other cooked pasta and enjoy with a glass of Sandhill Cabernet Sauvignon.

SERVES 4

SANDHILL WINERY
48313 North Sunset Road
Benton City
TEL: (360) 887-5629
sandhillwinery@aol.com

WINE SHOP, TOURS AND TASTINGS
Tasting room open 11 a.m.–5 p.m.
every weekend except Christmas and
New Year's Day.

GETTING THERE
Take Interstate 82 to Benton City exit
96. Follow SR 224 east about 1 mile
to Sunset Road. Take Sunset Road
north for 1½ miles.

WINERY HIGHLIGHTS
The winery also makes a Cinnamon
Teal Red Table Wine under the
Ridgefield label. The wine is named
after a duck found in the Ridgefield
National Wildlife Refuge. A portion
of the proceeds from the sale of this
wine is donated to the refuge.

# Silver Lake-Style Beef Daube

*featuring* SILVER LAKE SYRAH, COLUMBIA VALLEY

3 lb stewing beef, cut into cubes

3 Tbsp oil

1 cup chopped carrots

1 cup chopped onions

1 bulb fennel, chopped

3 cloves garlic, minced

1½ cups Syrah

1 can chopped tomatoes (15 oz)

2 strips orange peel (2 inches each)

½ tsp each dried thyme, ground cinnamon, ground cumin

1 bay leaf

1 tsp salt

¼ tsp freshly ground black pepper

2 Tbsp chopped parsley

½–1 cup beef stock

¼ cup dried currants (or substitute dark raisins)

2 cups black olives (8 oz can)

¼ cup toasted pine nuts

*Tasting room manager Ileene Case created this delicious recipe using Silver Lake Syrah. Dark, rich and intense, this wine demonstrates why Syrah is the bright new star in the Columbia Valley. The ripe flavors of raspberry, blackberry and other dark fruit mingle with aromas of white pepper and chocolate. The oak and vanilla characteristics added by aging in small French oak barrels enhance the overall complexity and depth of the lingering finish. This dish takes some time to prepare, but it's well worth the effort.*

*1.* Combine the beef, oil, vegetables, wine, tomatoes, orange peel, herbs and spices, bay leaf, salt, pepper and parsley in a large non-reactive bowl. Cover and marinate in the refrigerator for 12 hours.

*2.* Preheat the oven to 325°F. Transfer the contents of the bowl to a heatproof casserole dish or Dutch oven with a tight-fitting lid. Add enough beef stock to almost cover the contents of the casserole. Bring to a simmer on top of the stove, cover and transfer to the oven.

*3.* Cook for 3 hours, then add the currants and olives. Cook for another 30 minutes or until the meat falls apart when pierced with a fork.

*4.* Remove the orange peels. Sprinkle with toasted pine nuts before serving, and accompany with a glass of Silver Lake Syrah.

SERVES 4–6

## SILVER LAKE WINERY AT ROZA HILLS

1500 Vintage Road, Zillah
TEL: (509) 829-6235
FAX: (509) 829-6895
www.silverlakewinery.com
information@washingtonwine.com

### WINE SHOP, TOURS AND TASTINGS

Tasting room open daily Dec.–Mar.,
11 a.m.–4 p.m. and Apr.–Nov., 10 a.m.–
5 p.m. There are complimentary
tastings as well as reserve, library
and limited-release tastings for a
fee that's refundable with a wine
purchase.

### GETTING THERE

From I-82 take exit 52 toward Zillah.
Turn left on Cheyne Road then right
on Highland Drive. Turn left onto
Vintage Road and drive to the end of
the paved road. The driveway is on
the left.

### WINERY HIGHLIGHTS

Silver Lake has produced handcrafted premium varietal wines since
1989. The winery, tasting room,
picnic area and banquet room offer
unparalleled views of the lush
Yakima Valley.

# Townshend Cellar's Green Peppercorn Steak

*featuring* TOWNSHEND CHARDONNAY

4 New York steaks (8 oz each, about 1 inch thick)

½ tsp kosher or coarse salt

½ tsp freshly ground black pepper

6 Tbsp butter

¼ cup Chardonnay

1 heaped Tbsp Dijon mustard

½ cup whipping cream (or half-and-half)

2 Tbsp green peppercorns

*Don Townshend has come up with this awesome steak recipe using the Townshend Chardonnay. The 2004 vintage is 100 percent Chardonnay that was aged in American oak barrels for 6 months and underwent malolactic (secondary) fermentation. This recipe works equally well with lamb chops or chicken breasts.*

*1.* Season the steaks on all sides with salt and pepper. Heat a cast iron frying pan or heavy-bottomed pan over medium-high heat. Melt 2 Tbsp of the butter, being careful not to burn it. Add the steaks and sear for about 2 minutes on each side, shaking the pan constantly. Reduce the heat to medium and cook for an additional 2 minutes in total.

*2.* Remove the steaks from the pan and reduce the heat to medium or medium-low. Add the remaining 4 Tbsp butter, Chardonnay, mustard, cream and green peppercorns and bring to a simmer.

*3.* Return the steaks, along with any juices, to the pan and simmer for an additional 5 minutes (for medium rare), turning every 1–2 minutes. Remove the steaks and continue to cook the sauce for an additional 1–2 minutes, or until it is the consistency of yogurt. Add a bit more mustard and butter if necessary to balance the flavors.

*4.* To serve, pour the sauce over the steaks. Enjoy with a glass of Townshend Chardonnay and blow away the myth that white wine doesn't go with red meat.

SERVES 4

**TOWNSHEND CELLAR**

16112 North Greenbluff Road, Colbert

TEL: (509) 238-1400

FAX: (509) 238-6600

www.townshendcellar.com

jill@townshendcellar.com

WINE SHOP, TOURS AND TASTINGS
Open Fri.–Sun. noon–6 p.m. and other days by appointment.

GETTING THERE
From the west side follow Highway 395 to division "Y" and exit onto Highway 2. Go 5½ miles, then turn right on Day-Mt. Spokane Road. Follow for 1½ miles to Greenbluff Road and then turn left. The winery entrance is on the right. From the Spokane Valley, head north on Argonne/Bruce Road to the T-junction at Day-Mt. Spokane Road. Turn left, drive for ½ mile and turn right on Greenbluff Road.

WINERY HIGHLIGHTS
Try the unique huckleberry port-style wine when you visit!

# Walter Dacon Grilled Lamb Chops with Currant Sauce

*featuring* WALTER DACON C'EST SYRAH BELLE

8 lamb chops, fat trimmed off

2 Tbsp chopped fresh
   rosemary

3 medium shallots
   (2 chopped, 1 sliced)

5 Tbsp virgin olive oil

¼ cup dried currants

1 cup Syrah

1 cup chicken stock

1 Tbsp cassis liqueur

2 Tbsp butter

salt and freshly ground black
   pepper to taste

*Rick Hoonan has come up with this delicious lamb recipe using Walter Dacon C'est Syrah Belle, the softest, most feminine wine in their repertoire. The mouth feel is refined in its balance of soft, ripe blackberry fruit, nuanced oak sweetness and a lingering plummy tartness. The fruit flavors in the wine complement the currants to create a perfect sauce for the lamb.*

1. Combine the lamb, rosemary, chopped shallots, 3 Tbsp of the olive oil and pepper to taste in a resealable plastic bag. Ensure the meat is well coated and refrigerate for 4–8 hours.

2. Combine the currants and wine and infuse for 1 hour. Drain, setting aside the currants and placing the reserved wine in a saucepan over medium heat. Cook until the liquid has reduced by half. Add the chicken stock to the saucepan and reduce the liquid to ½ cup.

3. In a separate small pan heat the remaining 2 Tbsp of the olive oil over medium heat and sauté the sliced shallot until golden brown, around 4–5 minutes. Add the cooked shallots, cassis and wine-infused currants to the saucepan with the reduction. Reduce the heat to low and simmer until reduced to ¼ cup. Add the butter. Strain the sauce if desired (we prefer to serve it with the currants and shallots).

4. Remove the meat from the marinade and allow it to rest at room temperature for 30 minutes prior to grilling. Grill the lamb chops over high heat until the meat reaches 135°F for medium rare, about 2–3 minutes on each side. Let the meat rest for 10 minutes before serving.

5. Serve the lamb chops with the currant sauce and your favorite side dish accompanied by a glass of Walter Dacon C'est Syrah Belle.

SERVES 4

**WALTER DACON WINES**

50 SE Skookum Inlet Road, Shelton

TEL: (360) 426-5913

FAX: (360) 426-0523

www.walterdaconwines.com

winemaker@walterdaconwines.com

WINE SHOP, TOURS AND TASTINGS
Tasting room and wine shop open
Wed.–Sun. noon–6 p.m. Tours are
by request. Private tasting events by
appointment.

GETTING THERE
Head northbound from Olympia on
US 101. At mile marker 353 (Taylor
Station), turn right onto Lynch Road.
Proceed 1½ miles and turn right onto
Skookum Inlet Road.

WINERY HIGHLIGHTS
South Sound's newest winery and
tasting room is dedicated to Rhône
and Mediterranean varietals. Check
out the historic tasting bar, patio and
locally crafted culinary fare.

# Cabernet Franc

*pronounced (CA-BURR-NAY-FRAHNK)*

*DNA technology tells us that this varietal is actually
a genetic parent of Cabernet Sauvignon. It is one of
the famous grapes of Bordeaux in France and
historically was used primarily for blending. In North
America it's a common ingredient in the Meritage
(rhymes with heritage) blends, which are based on the
Bordeaux blends.*

*In Washington, Cabernet Franc is becoming popular as
a stand-alone wine in its own right, and winemakers
throughout the state seem to be planting more of this
varietal each year. In France, it is often used to make
rosé-style wine but here it is generally turned into a
medium-bodied red, softer and with less tannin than a
Cabernet Sauvignon.*

*The grapes are thinner skinned and ripen earlier than
Cabernet Sauvignon. They are able to survive cold
winters but don't withstand sudden frosts well.*

*The wine has a fairly good aging potential. Flavors of
blueberry, cherry and blackcurrant are common, as are
aromas of mild coffee, fresh tobacco and stone fruits.
This wine is popular with vegetarians as it goes so well
with hearty vegetables, such as zucchini, carrot and
pumpkin, and it's a great match for vegetarian lasagna.
It also pairs surprisingly well with white meats, salmon
and tuna.*

# Windy Point Vineyard's Apple Wood-Smoked Pork Loin Sandwich

*featuring* WINDY POINT ESTATE CABERNET FRANC

2 lb apple wood chips

1½ cups Cabernet Franc

¼ cup sugar

4-6 lb pork loin

2 Tbsp steak seasoning

pickled red onions and chipotle mayonnaise (optional)

1 loaf crusty bread (ciabatta, focaccia or your favorite loaf)

8 oz Gouda cheese (smoked if you like)

*This recipe by Chef "Big John" Caudill was created to complement the spicy richness of the Windy Point Cabernet Franc with its notes of black pepper and raspberry. The perfect red wine for a summer night on the deck! This estate wine was grown and produced in the Yakima Valley, where Cabernet Franc has gained a reputation for excellence.*

1.  Soak the wood chips in the wine for at least 2 hours. Drain the wood chips and set aside, reserving the wine. Bring the wine to a boil with the sugar in a small saucepan and reduce until it has a syrupy consistency.

2.  Remove the pork from the fridge so it can sit at room temperature for 30 minutes prior to cooking. Preheat the grill to high. Place a smoking tray with the hydrated chips on 1 side of the grill, close the lid and let burn for 5 minutes. (If your grill does not have a smoking tray, use a small foil tray or make envelopes from foil.)

3.  Sprinkle the pork with the steak seasoning and place on the opposite side of the grill from the wood chips. Close the lid and sear each side for 1–2 minutes, until distinct grill marks appear. Once the pork has been seared on both sides, turn off the burners on that side of the grill to give the meat a slow, smoke-roasted flavor. If you have a meat thermometer with a long probe and digital readout, insert it in the middle of the pork at this point and set the temperature to 155°F. Let the chips burn on high for another 15 minutes, then reduce the heat to medium-low. Different grills will provide different results, so rely on the meat temperature.

4. While the pork is cooking, periodically baste it with the wine reduction, creating a beautiful mahogany crust. This may take up to 2 hours, depending on the heat of your grill. The wine-soaked wood and the wine glaze impart a sweet, smoky character to the meat.

5. When the pork has reached 155°F remove it from the grill and cover loosely with foil. Slice the bread and toast until lightly browned. Layer 1 side of each slice with Gouda and let melt slightly. Fill the sandwiches with sliced pork (Big John also suggests pickled red onions and chipotle mayonnaise as fillings) and toast in a moderate oven or under a grill for another 4–5 minutes or until warmed through. Enjoy this sandwich on the deck with your favorite green or pasta salad and a glass of Windy Point Estate Cabernet Franc.

SERVES 4 WITH PLENTY OF LEFTOVERS!

# Woodhouse Family Cellars Syrah Beef Fillets

*featuring* WOODHOUSE FAMILY CELLARS KENNEDY SHAH SYRAH

6 Tbsp butter

1–2 cloves garlic, minced

3 Tbsp finely chopped shallots

3 Tbsp finely chopped green
onions

2 cups mushrooms

1 cup beef broth (organic is
best)

1 cup Syrah

1½ tsp Worcestershire sauce

4 beef fillets (8–10 oz each)

freshly ground black pepper
and gourmet steak
seasoning to taste

*Easy to make and delicious to eat: what more could you ask for? The wine used in this recipe has a powerful dark berry fruit dressed in a cloak of rose petals and earthy mushrooms. A subtle yet complex nose explodes on the palate with soft, round tannins.*

1. Melt the butter in a large frying pan over medium heat and sauté the garlic, shallots, scallions and mushrooms until tender, about 10 minutes. Add the broth, wine and Worcestershire sauce and bring to a boil. Reduce the heat and simmer for 15 minutes, until the sauce reduces by half.

2. Heat the grill to medium-high. Generously sprinkle the fillets with pepper and steak seasoning, rubbing in well. Grill the fillets to your liking (5–6 minutes each side for medium rare). Serve the fillets with the sauce overtop. Enjoy!

SERVES 4

## WOODHOUSE FAMILY CELLARS/ KENNEDY SHAH

15500 Woodinville Redmond Road
NE Ste C600, Woodinville
TEL: (425) 527-0608
FAX: (425) 527-0609
www.woodhousefamilycellars.com
abbey@woodhouse-usa.com

WINE SHOP, TOURS AND TASTINGS
Tasting room open Fri. noon–
4 p.m. and Sat.–Sun. noon–5 p.m., or
throughout the week by appointment.

GETTING THERE
The winery is well signposted. When
you get to the "Y" intersection at
the bottom of the hill on 143rd
Street, take a left onto Woodinville-
Redmond Road NE and follow for
½ mile. The winery is on the right.

WINERY HIGHLIGHTS
Woodhouse Family Cellars has
5 individual labels, including Merlot,
Syrah, Bordeaux Blend, Muscat and
a Picnic Blend.

# Barnard Griffin Beef with Shallots, Pancetta and Port

*featuring* BARNARD GRIFFIN PORT

1½ lb shallots, peeled and
    halved lengthwise

salt and freshly ground black
    pepper to taste

3 Tbsp olive oil

1½ cups port

6 cups beef broth

1 Tbsp tomato paste

8 slices pancetta

2–3 lb beef tenderloin

½ cup fresh thyme, chopped

1½ Tbsp butter

¼ cup all-purpose flour

*Great port is about perfectly ripened fruit, and the red variety that ripens best in Washington is Syrah. This wine is similar in structure to vintage-style ports, but the fruit-forward character makes it a satisfying glass even when consumed young. The rich flavor makes an elegant sauce that makes this meal suitable for the fanciest of dinner parties.*

1. Preheat the oven to 350°F. Place the shallots and oil in a baking dish, toss to coat and season with salt and pepper. Roast 30–40 minutes or until the shallots are deep brown and tender, stirring occasionally. Remove from the oven and set aside.

2. Boil the port and broth in a saucepan until reduced by half, about 30 minutes. Whisk in the tomato paste. Set aside.

3. In a large roasting pan over medium heat, sauté the pancetta until golden. Remove and drain on paper towels.

4. Pat the beef dry and sprinkle with thyme, salt and pepper. Place in a roasting pan and brown on all sides over medium-high heat, about 2–3 minutes per side. Transfer the pan to the oven and roast until a meat thermometer registers 130–140°F for medium rare, about 45 minutes. Transfer the beef to a platter and cover loosely with foil.

## BARNARD GRIFFIN WINERY

878 Tulip Lane, Richland
TEL: (509) 627-0266
FAX: (509) 627-7776
www.barnardgriffin.com
kim@barnardgriffin.com

### WINE SHOP, TOURS AND TASTINGS
Open for tastings daily 10 a.m.–6 p.m.

### GETTING THERE
When driving toward the Tri-Cities east on I-182, take exit 3 and turn right onto Queensgate Drive. Take an immediate left onto Columbia Park Trail, then another left onto Windmill Road. Veer to the right onto Tulip Lane. Barnard Griffin is the second winery on the right.

### WINERY HIGHLIGHTS
Founded in 1983 by Rob Griffin and Deborah Barnard, Barnard Griffin has been producing award-winning wines for over 20 years.

**5.** Spoon the fat off the top of the pan drippings. Place the roasting pan over high heat. Add the reduced broth mixture and bring to a boil, scraping up any browned bits from the bottom of the pan. Transfer the liquid to a medium saucepan and bring to a simmer.

**6.** Mix the butter and flour together in a bowl to form a paste. Whisk the paste into the broth and simmer until the sauce thickens. Stir in the roasted shallots and reserved pancetta.

**7.** Cut the beef into ½-inch slices and spoon the sauce overtop. Serve with roasted vegetables and Barnard Griffin Merlot. Follow dinner with a glass of Barnard Griffin Port and some blue cheese.

SERVES 4–6

# Vegetarian

Rice is born in water and must die in wine.

— *Italian proverb about risotto*

# Kiona Vineyards Goat Cheese-Stuffed Lemberger Portobellos

*featuring* KIONA LEMBERGER

3 fresh large portobello
  mushrooms (4–5 inches)

3 Tbsp butter

1 Tbsp olive oil

¾ cup Lemberger

salt and freshly ground black
  pepper to taste

2 cloves garlic, minced

½ cup chopped fresh shallots

1 package frozen chopped
  spinach (10 oz), thawed and
  drained

4 oz soft goat cheese

3 Tbsp grated Parmesan
  cheese

⅔ cup whipping cream

¾ cup shredded goat Gouda
  (or other semi-hard goat
  cheese)

5 Tbsp chopped fresh basil

*The first commercial Lemberger in the entire United States was released here in 1983. It has a spicy, intriguing background with well-defined aromas of blackberry and cloves. It is mildly tannic and has great flavors with a velvety mouth feel. Heavier-textured and -flavored mushrooms like portobellos and chanterelles go very well with Lemberger.*

1. Preheat the oven to 400°F. Lightly coat an ovenproof pan that will hold the mushrooms without overlapping with cooking spray and set it aside. Trim the mushroom stems and clean the caps with a damp towel.

2. Melt 1 Tbsp of the butter into the olive oil in a large frying pan over medium-high heat. Add the wine and bring to a simmer. Add the mushrooms, cap side down, and cook over medium heat for 5 minutes. Turn the mushrooms over, season with salt and pepper and cook 5 minutes more. Transfer the mushrooms, gills facing up, to the prepared pan. Set aside the frying pan with the wine/mushroom liquid.

3. Melt 1 Tbsp of the butter in a separate frying pan and sauté the garlic until just golden. Reduce the heat to medium-low, add the shallots and cook until soft, about 5 minutes. Add the spinach and soft goat cheese and stir until it is well combined and the cheese has melted. Season with salt and pepper. Spoon the spinach mixture evenly over the mushroom caps and sprinkle with Parmesan cheese.

**KIONA VINEYARDS AND WINERY**

44612 North Sunset Road

Benton City

TEL: (509) 588-6716

FAX: (509) 588-3219

www.kionawine.com

info@kionawine.com

WINE SHOP, TOURS AND TASTINGS

Open daily noon–5 p.m. except on major holidays.

GETTING THERE

From I-82 take exit 96 to Highway 224 east (W. Richland). Travel 1½ miles on 224, then turn north (left) on Sunset Road. The winery is 1 mile off the highway on the left.

WINERY HIGHLIGHTS

A brand new tasting room and barrel storage facility, sweeping views and an open patio complement a world-class array of wines.

**4.** Add the last Tbsp of the butter to the frying pan with the wine/mushroom liquid. Melt over medium-low heat and stir, scraping the browned bits from the bottom of the pan. Add the cream and stir until slightly thickened, about 5 minutes. Pour the sauce into the pan with the mushrooms, but not overtop of the mushrooms. Gently lift each mushroom so the sauce covers the entire surface of the pan. Sprinkle the mushrooms with the shredded Gouda and bake for 15 minutes or until the cheese is slightly golden. Remove the mushrooms from the oven, sprinkle with basil and let cool for 5 minutes. Quarter each mushroom and serve with a dollop of the sauce on the side.

SERVES 6–8

# Vegetarian Chili

¼ cup dried green lentils

2 Tbsp olive oil

1 cup chopped onion

2 cloves garlic, crushed

1 cup chopped red bell pepper

2 carrots, thinly sliced

¾ cup chopped celery

¾ cup red wine

1 can chopped tomatoes
    (15 oz)

1 can corn (8–10 oz)

2 cans kidney beans, drained
    and rinsed (15 oz each)

½ tsp sugar

2 Tbsp chili powder

½ tsp cayenne pepper

1 tsp paprika

salt and freshly ground black
    pepper to taste

*Vegetarian chili is so versatile. It can be enjoyed on rice, on baked potatoes, in tacos, on veggie dogs or on its own. The wine gives the chili a fuller flavor. Leftovers are always delicious and it freezes well. What more could you want from a meal?*

1. Place the lentils in a small saucepan, cover with water and simmer for about 45 minutes. Drain and set aside.

2. Heat the olive oil in a frying pan over medium-high heat and sauté the onion, garlic, red pepper, carrots and celery. Allow to cook for 5–6 minutes. Add the presoaked lentils, wine, tomatoes with their juice, corn, beans, sugar, chili powder, cayenne pepper and paprika. Bring to a simmer for 45 minutes. Season with salt and pepper.

SERVES 4–6

# Asparagus and Goat Cheese Parcels

*This is one of our all-time favorite vegetarian dishes. The flavorful filling wrapped up in flaky pastry and served in a pool of wine and citrus butter makes an impressive presentation. Puff pastry is very easy to use, so don't be intimidated by it.*

1 lb asparagus, woody ends removed

4 oz soft goat cheese at room temperature

2 cloves garlic, crushed

salt to taste

½ cup all-purpose flour

1 package puff pastry (14 oz)

1 egg

1 Tbsp milk

½ cup white wine

2 Tbsp lemon juice

¾ cup cold butter, cubed

1.  Bring a large pot of lightly salted water to a boil. Add the asparagus and cook for about 3 minutes, until just tender. Immediately remove from the boiling water and plunge into a bowl or sink of ice water. When the asparagus is cold to the touch, remove it to paper towels and pat dry. Divide into 4 bunches.

2.  In a small bowl, mix the goat cheese and garlic. Taste, and if necessary, add salt.

3.  On a lightly floured surface, roll the puff pastry into 8 equal rectangles a little longer and wider than the asparagus bundles. Place 1 bunch of asparagus on 1 rectangle and top with ¼ of the goat cheese mixture. Wet the edges of the pastry with water, place another rectangle on top and press the edges to seal, making an enclosed package. Trim any excess pastry. Repeat to make 3 more parcels.

4.  Beat the egg and milk together in a small bowl. Brush the top and sides of each parcel with the egg mixture. Place the parcels on a lightly greased baking sheet and bake for 15–20 minutes or until the pastry is golden brown.

5.  Combine the wine and lemon juice in a small heavy saucepan. Bring to a boil, then simmer over medium heat until the liquid is reduced to about ¼ cup. Reduce the heat to low. Add the butter cube by cube, whisking the whole time.

6.  Serve the asparagus parcels on a pool of sauce.

SERVES 4

# Mediterranean Pizza

1 cup warm water

2 tsp sugar

2 tsp active dry yeast

3 Tbsp olive oil

5 cloves garlic, crushed

2 tsp dried Italian seasoning

1 tsp salt

2½ cups all-purpose flour

½ onion, diced

salt and freshly ground black
    pepper to taste

1 can chopped tomatoes
    (28 oz)

¾ cup red wine

⅓ cup chopped black olives

⅓ cup crumbled feta

⅓ cup sun-dried tomatoes,
    excess oil removed

⅓ cup chopped fresh basil
    leaves

1 cup grated mozzarella cheese

*Everybody loves pizza. This recipe gives you everything from the crispy thin crust right through to the rich tomato sauce and toppings. This makes two thin-crust pizzas. If you only want one, freeze the leftover pizza dough. Just rub some olive oil over the dough ball and place it in a freezer bag.*

1.  Mix the water and 1 tsp of the sugar in a medium-sized bowl. Sprinkle the yeast overtop and let it sit for about 10 minutes. Add 2 Tbsp of the olive oil, 2 of the crushed garlic cloves, the Italian seasoning, salt and flour. Combine to form a soft dough. Knead for about 5 minutes, until you have a smooth, stiff dough. Add a bit more flour if necessary to prevent sticking. Cover with a clean cloth and let rise in a warm place for 25–30 minutes.

2.  Heat the remaining 1 Tbsp of the olive oil in a large pan over medium heat. Add the onion and sauté for about 5 minutes, stirring frequently. Add the remaining 3 cloves of crushed garlic and lightly season with salt and pepper. Continue to sauté for another 2 minutes.

3.  Add the tomatoes with their juice and increase the heat to high. Cook, stirring frequently for about 10 minutes or until the liquid has mostly evaporated. Reduce the heat to medium-high, then add the wine and remaining 1 tsp of sugar. Cook for about 15–20 minutes, until the liquid has evaporated.

4. Put half the tomato mixture in a blender or food processor and blend until smooth. Mix with the unblended tomato mixture.

5. Preheat the oven to 425°F. Lightly grease 2 medium pizza pans and divide the dough in half. Place the dough on the pans and press it out with your fingers to make the pizza base.

6. Spread the tomato sauce over the dough, dividing it evenly between the 2 pans. Distribute the olives, feta, sun-dried tomatoes, basil and mozzarella over the 2 pizzas. Bake for about 20 minutes, until the crust is crisp and the cheese is bubbly.

SERVES 4–6

CHEF'S SHORTCUT

*If you're short on time, use a store-bought pizza crust or pita bread. For a quicker and easier sauce, heat 1 tsp of olive oil in a small saucepan over medium heat and sauté 3 crushed garlic cloves. Stir in 1 can of tomato paste (5.5 oz), add ¾ cup red wine and simmer for about 20 minutes.*

# Wawawai Canyon Fondue

*featuring* WAWAWAI CANYON GEWÜRZTRAMINER

1 lb Cougar Gold (or Swiss) cheese, grated

½ lb Gruyère cheese, grated

3 Tbsp all-purpose flour

1 tsp grated whole nutmeg

½ tsp ground white pepper

1¼ cups Wawawai Canyon Gewürztraminer

2 large cloves garlic, finely minced

cubed baguette, Asian pear wedges or steamed asparagus for dipping

*Wawawai Canyon Gewürztraminer is produced exclusively from fruit grown on the Wahluke Slope, designated the eighth Washington appellation in January 2006. It is one of the hottest, driest grape-growing regions in the state, allowing the grapes to ripen early and attain higher sugar levels. If you are fond of cold-climate Gewürztraminer, prepare to be surprised by the unique flavors of this vintage. Look for a rounder, full-bodied wine, with aromas of cinnamon and ripe pear. The spicy overtones in the wine marry exceptionally well with the sharpness of the Cougar Gold and Gruyère cheese in this delightful fondue. For this recipe you will require a fondue pot with long-handled forks.*

1.  Combine the cheeses, flour, nutmeg and white pepper in a large bowl. Toss well.

2.  Place ¼ cup of the wine in a 2-quart heavy saucepan and gently cook the garlic, taking care to keep it from browning. Add the remaining wine and bring it to a simmer over low heat.

3.  Add the cheese mixture by handfuls, whisking constantly until the cheese is melted and smooth, about 5 minutes. Serve in a fondue pot with your favorite accompaniments.

SERVES 8—10

**WAWAWAI CANYON WINERY**

5602 State Route 270, Pullman

TEL: (509) 336-9316

www.wawawaicanyon.com

chavens@wawawaicanyon.com

WINE SHOP, TOURS AND TASTINGS
Please call or check the website for
current hours.

GETTING THERE
The winery is located 18 miles south
of Pullman and roughly 2 miles from
the Snake River on State Route 270.

WINERY HIGHLIGHTS
The tasting room is in a restored
dairy barn that shares its lot with
a premium nursery. The spacious
barn is also home to an art gallery
featuring paintings and sculptures by
local artist Christine Havens. There
is a picnic ground where guests can
relax, enjoy the scenery and listen to
live music.

# Gewürztraminer

*pronounced (*GAA-VERTS-TRA-MEE-NER*)*

*Wine historians disagree on the meaning and origins
of the word Gewürztraminer. However, most report
that the name comes from* **gewurz**, *a German word
meaning "spicy" and* **Traminer**, *which is a variety of
grape.*

*Traminer comes from the Italian village of Termeno,
located in Germany's Tyrolean Alps. The grape had
been growing very successfully there since the Middle
Ages. Sometime in the last few hundred years it mutated
into the grape we know as Gewürztraminer. Today it's
commonly grown in the Alsace region of France.*

*This variety has always done well in Washington
because it's hardy enough to withstand most frosts. It
has distinct aromatic characteristics of flowers and spicy
perfumes, similar to Muscat.*

*Washington winemakers have been more experimental
with this grape than the rest of the world, and they
are producing dry, off-dry and sweet wines. The wine
can be stored for a few years without problems, but
it's best when consumed young. Gewürztraminer is a
great accompaniment for a wide variety of foods. It is
especially good with spicy foods, stone fruits, game,
poultry and cheese.*

# Baked Red Peppers Stuffed with Zucchini Risotto

*featuring* VIOGNIER

6 large red bell peppers

2 Tbsp olive oil

½ cup butter

3 medium zucchini, diced

½ cup chopped parsley

6-7 cups vegetable stock

2 onions, finely chopped

2 cloves garlic, crushed

1½ cups arborio rice

1 cup Viognier

1½ cups grated Parmesan cheese

*Two wonderful vegetables combined with creamy risotto and topped with Parmesan cheese. Although these vegetables can be found in any supermarket year-round, Washington-grown zucchini is usually available between July and September, and Washington-grown bell peppers during August and September.*

1. Preheat the oven to 350°F. Cut the tops off the peppers and remove the seeds and membranes. Place the peppers on a baking tray and drizzle with the olive oil. Bake for about 15–20 minutes, until they are just soft. Set aside.

2. Melt ¼ cup of the butter in a frying pan over medium heat. Add the zucchini and sauté for 5 minutes. Add the parsley and remove from the heat.

3. Bring the vegetable stock to a simmer in a medium saucepan. In a separate, large saucepan melt the remaining ¼ cup butter over medium heat. Add the onions and garlic and sauté for 2–3 minutes. Add the rice and stir for 1–2 minutes. Add the wine and keep stirring until it has all been absorbed, about 4–5 minutes.

4. When the wine is all absorbed start adding the stock, about ¾ cup at a time, stirring constantly. When the stock has been absorbed, add more and continue stirring. It should take about 18–20 minutes. The rice should be creamy but firm in the middle. You may have to use a little more or less of the stock depending on the rice. Add the sautéed zucchini and ½ the cheese and stir well. Spoon the risotto into the baked peppers and top with the remaining cheese.

5. Bake in the oven for 10 minutes before serving.

SERVES 6

# Side Dishes

Nothing would be more tiresome than
eating or drinking if God had not made
them a pleasure as well as a necessity.

—*Voltaire*

# Basel Cellars Cabernet Ragout of Chanterelles, Favas and Peas with Oil-Poached Tomatoes

*featuring* BASEL CELLARS PHEASANT RUN VINEYARD ESTATE CABERNET SAUVIGNON

1 pint cherry tomatoes
(heirloom or Sungold are
preferred)

2 cloves garlic, sliced

1 shallot, thinly sliced

2 bay leaves

3 sprigs thyme, chopped

¾ cup Cabernet Sauvignon

1 cup extra virgin olive oil

1½ cups shucked English peas

1½ cups fava beans

1½ cups small summer
chanterelles, brushed clean

2 Tbsp butter

½ cup peeled red pearl onions,
halved vertically

3 cups hearty chicken stock

3 sprigs tarragon, chopped

3 sprigs marjoram, chopped

2 Tbsp chopped mint

salt and freshly ground black
pepper to taste

*Both this dish and the wine would be magnificent with grilled lamb chops. The wine is no fruit bomb. It relies on its earthy structure to provide the framework for dark fruit flavors of plum and blackberry. Green tea and mint help flesh out the mid-palate. The finish is long and expressive, swimming in an ocean of silky tannins.*

*1.* Preheat the oven to 300°F. Place the tomatoes in a small baking dish with the garlic, shallot, bay leaves, thyme, ½ cup of the wine and olive oil (reserve 3 Tbsp). Season with salt. Bake for 20 minutes and set aside.

*2.* Bring salted water to a boil in a saucepan over high heat. Prepare a bowl of salted ice water and set aside. When the water is boiling, blanch the peas for 30 seconds. Using a slotted spoon, transfer to the ice water to arrest the cooking process. Add the favas to the boiling water and blanch for 1 minute, then transfer to the ice water. Peel the outer membrane or skin off the favas to reveal the bean.

*3.* Heat the reserved 3 Tbsp of oil in a sauté pan over medium-high heat and sauté the chanterelles for about 3 minutes, until they are golden brown and have released their moisture. Stir, tossing often to prevent burning. Season lightly with salt and pepper. Add the remaining ¼ cup of wine and cook until it's reduced by half. Remove from the heat and set aside.

*4.* Melt 1 Tbsp of the butter in a saucepan over medium heat, add the onions and sauté for 3 minutes. Season with salt and pepper. Add the chicken stock and simmer 3 more minutes. Add the chanterelles and remaining 1 Tbsp butter and cook for 2 minutes. Finish by adding the favas, peas and herbs.

**5.** Transfer to a bowl and season with salt and pepper. Add the tomatoes and some of the poaching liquid. Serve immediately.

SERVES 4

BASEL CELLARS
2901 Old Milton Highway
Walla Walla
TEL: (509) 522-0200
FAX: (509) 522-0996
www.baselcellars.com
info@baselcellars.com

WINE SHOP, TOURS AND TASTINGS
Open Mon.-Sat. 10 a.m.-4 p.m. and
Sun. 11 a.m.-4 p.m. Closed on Sun.
during the off season. Call for details.
A $5 tasting fee is refundable with
your wine purchase.

GETTING THERE
Follow South 9th Avenue until it
becomes Highway 125. Keep heading
south on Highway 125 toward Milton
Freewater, then turn right onto the
Old Milton Highway. Basel Cellars is
almost 1 mile up on your left.

WINERY HIGHLIGHTS
Basel Cellars occupies 85 acres
overlooking the Walla Walla River
with vistas of wheat-covered
foothills and the Blue Mountains.
The Estate features luxury overnight
accommodations for up to 18 guests
and the location is ideal for corporate
meetings and retreats.

# Baked Fennel with Parmesan

**2 medium fennel bulbs,
trimmed and halved
lengthwise**

**½ Tbsp olive oil**

**2 cloves garlic, crushed**

**½ cup white wine**

**¼ cup grated Parmesan cheese**

*This makes an unusual side dish that goes well with a lot of
different foods but is especially suited to Italian dishes. It has
been shown that eating fennel actually helps digestion, so
instead of using antacids, add some fennel to your diet!*

1. Preheat the oven to 350°F. Place the fennel in a baking
   dish flat side down.

2. Combine the olive oil, garlic and wine in a small bowl and
   mix well.

3. Pour the mixture over the fennel bulbs, cover and bake
   for 45 minutes, turning once during the cooking process.
   Remove the fennel from the oven and sprinkle the flat side
   with Parmesan cheese.

4. Place under the broiler until the cheese is golden brown.

   SERVES 4

# Asparagus in White Wine

*How is it possible to improve on the taste of fresh asparagus?*
*Serve it in a white wine and butter sauce! A little-known fact*
*about asparagus is that it is actually a member of the lily*
*family. An asparagus plant will continue to produce spears*
*for as many as 25 years.*

**1 lb asparagus**
**½ cup white wine**
**2 Tbsp butter**
**salt and freshly ground black**
**   pepper to taste**

*1.* Break off the woody ends of the asparagus. Prepare a
steamer (or colander) over boiling water and steam the
asparagus just until tender, about 5–7 minutes. Do not
overcook.

*2.* While the asparagus is steaming, cook the wine in a large
frying pan over medium-high heat until it's reduced by
half. Take the pan off the heat and add the butter a bit at a
time while stirring.

*3.* Transfer the asparagus to the frying pan and coat well in
the sauce. Reheat over medium heat if necessary. Season
with salt and pepper.

SERVES 4

# Chelangr'La Sautéed Mushrooms

*featuring* CHELANGR'LA SEMILLON

3 Tbsp butter

2 lb mushrooms

⅓ cup Semillon

generous dash Worcestershire
  sauce, or to taste

salt and freshly ground black
  pepper to taste

¼ cup sour cream

*This fruity, crisp wine complements Greek and Italian dishes, seafood and spicy foods, such as Mexican cuisine. Serve it slightly chilled. Here it provides extra flavor in this magnificent mushroom recipe.*

1. Melt the butter in a frying pan over medium-high heat. Add the mushrooms, wine, Worcestershire sauce, salt and pepper. Push the mushrooms around the frying pan so they are well coated. Bring to a boil and as the liquid evaporates, pull the mushrooms to 1 side so the liquid does not boil all the way down. Periodically, return the mushrooms to the liquid so they are coated and then pull them away again.

2. When the liquid has evaporated, stir in the sour cream. Reduce the heat and continue stirring until the moisture is gone. The mushrooms should be slightly seared and coated with glazing. These mushrooms make an excellent accompaniment to steak. They would also be a great addition to your breakfast plate.

SERVES 6

## CHELANGR'LA WINERY

3310 Manson Boulevard, Manson

TEL: (509) 687-9746

www.chelangrla.com

chelangrla@aol.com

### WINE SHOP, TOURS AND TASTINGS
Tasting room open daily Apr. 1–Nov. 1.
Open weekends year-round. Tours
are available.

### GETTING THERE
Drive through Manson and follow
the signs.

### WINERY HIGHLIGHTS
Chelangr'La is the smallest winery
in the valley and the only one that
produces fruit wines. They feature
a 100 percent raspberry and a 100
percent elderberry wine as well as
the grape varietals.

### WINERY SPECIAL OFFER
The winery will provide free stem
jewelry when you show your copy of
this book.

# Braised Garlic Mash

½ Tbsp olive oil

1 medium-sized head garlic, cloves separated and peeled

½ cup white wine

2 lb red potatoes, peeled and chopped

¼ cup whipping cream

½ cup butter

nutmeg, salt and freshly ground black pepper to taste

*Mashed potatoes are great, garlic mashed potatoes even greater, but braised garlic mashed potatoes are the greatest. This dish could change the way you think about mashed potatoes forever. Do not allow the potatoes to cool before you mash them or they will become gluey.*

1. Heat the olive oil in a small saucepan over medium-low heat. When the oil is hot, add the whole garlic cloves and brown for 2–3 minutes. Add the wine and simmer until it evaporates, about 20 minutes. If the wine evaporates before 20 minutes has passed, add a little more. Remove from the heat.

2. While the garlic is simmering, cook the potatoes in a large pot of boiling salted water until they are tender, about 10–15 minutes.

3. Drain the potatoes. Add the cream, butter and garlic. Mash until fluffy using a potato masher or, for extra creamy potatoes, an electric mixer (be careful not to overbeat). Add nutmeg, salt and pepper to taste.

Serves 4

# Grilled Vegetable Skewers

*These wine-marinated vegetable skewers are an exciting alternative to the traditional salad you'd normally find at a barbecue. They'll be snapped up quickly by vegetarians and meat lovers alike, so you may need to double the recipe.*

*1.* Place the vegetables in a large non-metallic dish or resealable plastic bag.

*2.* Mix the oil, wine, lemon juice, garlic and chives in a small jar or airtight container. Shake vigorously until well combined. Pour the marinade over the vegetables, cover or seal and refrigerate for 2 hours, stirring occasionally.

*3.* Thread the vegetables onto metal or bamboo skewers. (If using bamboo, presoak the skewers in water for about 30 minutes.) Cook on a preheated, lightly greased grill for about 10 minutes, turning occasionally, until the vegetables are tender. To add more flavor, brush with marinade while cooking.

*4.* Lightly sprinkle with salt and freshly ground pepper before serving.

SERVES 4

8 cherry tomatoes

8 medium mushrooms

2 red bell peppers, cut in bite-sized pieces

2 medium zucchinis, cut in bite-sized pieces

1 large purple onion, cut in bite-sized pieces

¼ cup olive oil

¼ cup white wine

1 Tbsp lemon juice

1 clove garlic, crushed

¼ cup finely chopped chives

salt and freshly ground black pepper to taste

# Canoe Ridge Walla Walla Sweets

*featuring* CANOE RIDGE MERLOT

5 medium sweet onions
   (Walla Walla)

2 cups Merlot

freshly ground black pepper
   to taste

2 Tbsp olive oil

*This is a terrific recipe for the grill or even a campfire. It's unusual but the results are fantastic and you'll fascinate your dinner guests. The Canoe Ridge Merlot is fermented in small lots and aged in 75 percent French and 25 percent American oak for 14–16 months. The Merlot is an elegant supple wine with the finesse of a Pinot Noir and lush characteristics of raspberry, dark cherry and Belgian chocolate.*

1. Cut the tops and bottoms off the onions to flatten them. Remove the outer layers of skin. With a paring knife, carefully cut away some of the middle of each onion to make a reservoir for the Merlot.

2. Place each onion on its own piece of foil. Make sure the foil is large enough to completely wrap the onion. Fill each onion with the wine and grind some pepper overtop. Drizzle the olive oil on the outer layer of each onion and wrap in foil to seal in the liquid ingredients. You may want to add a second layer of foil.

3. Place the onions on the grill for about 30 minutes. Test for doneness by squeezing them. When they are cooked they will be soft and supple. Larger onions will need more cooking time and small onions will not take the entire 30 minutes.

4. Carefully open the top of the foil to vent the steam and allow to cool a bit before serving. Handle with caution as they will be very hot and hold their heat for some time, especially when left in the foil.

SERVES 5

## CANOE RIDGE VINEYARD

1102 West Cherry Street, Walla Walla
TEL: (509) 527-0885
FAX: (509) 527-0886
www.canoeridgevineyard.com
crvinfo@canoeridgevineyard.com

WINE SHOP, TOURS AND TASTINGS
Tasting room open daily May–Sep.,
11 a.m.–5 p.m., Oct.–Apr., 11 a.m.–
4 p.m. Closed major holidays and
Dec. 24–Jan. 1.

GETTING THERE
Coming from the west, when you get
to Walla Walla turn right onto West
Pine Street and then right onto Irene
Street. Irene Street becomes West
Cherry Street.

WINERY HIGHLIGHTS
The estate vineyard overlooks
Umatilla National Wildlife Refuge.
This is a popular nesting area for
Great Basin Canada geese, ducks and
many other marsh and water birds.

# Sauces & Marinades

Wine is light held together by water.

—*Galileo*

# Waterbrook Winery Summer Grove Marinade for Chicken

*featuring* WB Primarius Sauvignon Blanc

½ cup Sauvignon Blanc

½ cup orange juice (no pulp)

1 Tbsp aged balsamic vinegar

1 Tbsp Worcestershire sauce

2 Tbsp stone-ground mustard

3 Tbsp grapeseed oil (garlic-infused if possible, such as Salute Santé!)

3 Tbsp orange marmalade (optional)

*WB is a new label/line for Waterbrook Winery. They have made many Sauvignon Blancs over the years, but the WB Primarius is a limited-case production (less than 350 cases) that combines the purest premium fruit. This is 100 percent Sauvignon Blanc that's perfectly balanced with lively acidity and clean, crisp characteristics.*

1. Mix all the ingredients together in a bowl, then transfer to an airtight container or covered non-reactive pan. Place the chicken in the container and shake to coat it thoroughly with the marinade.

2. Cover and refrigerate overnight, shaking 2–3 times at intervals to recoat the chicken.

3. It's also a good idea to season the chicken with a little bit of lemon pepper before cooking.

MAKES 1½–2 CUPS (ENOUGH FOR 4–6 BREASTS)

## WATERBROOK WINERY

Tasting Room is at 31 East Main
Street, Walla Walla
TEL: (509) 529-1262
FAX: (509) 529-4770
www.waterbrook.com
info@waterbrook.com

### WINE SHOP, TOURS AND TASTINGS

The tasting room/gallery is located in
the historic center of downtown Walla
Walla. Tasting is free to the public for
groups of fewer than 20 people. Open
daily 10:30am–4:30 p.m.

### GETTING THERE

From Seattle take I-90 eastbound.
Directly after Ellensburg take the I-82
eastbound exit through Yakima/Tri
Cities. Turn left at the Highway 395/
Highway 12 junction and continue
through Touchet and Lowden. Take
the 2nd Avenue exit. Turn right on
2nd Avenue and left on Main Street.

### WINERY HIGHLIGHTS

Waterbrook is the fourth-oldest
winery and one of the largest private
producers in the Walla Walla Valley,
which now boasts over 80 wineries.

### WINERY SPECIAL OFFER

If you show your copy of this book
you will receive an incredible $15
off your bottle of WB Primarius
Sauvignon Blanc when visiting
the tasting room! While stock
is available.

# Sauvignon Blanc

*pronounced (*SO-VIN-YAWN-BLAHN*)*

*Wine historians seem to agree that the Loire River
Valley in France is the home of Sauvignon Blanc. The
grape has a long history in this region and many wine
lovers feel the Loire River wines set the benchmark for
all Sauvignon Blanc producers.*

*Sauvignon Blanc is also widely known as Fumé Blanc, a
successful marketing term coined by Robert Mondavi of
California's Robert Mondavi winery. This variety grows
in many unlikely places around the world, including
Israel and Texas.*

*In Washington the variety has continued to increase in
popularity largely due to its quality of pairing well with
so many foods. Washington Sauvignon Blancs tend to be
dry and full of fruit. They are commonly blended with
Semillon, and in many ways are similar to the white
wines of Bordeaux.*

*This wine is well known for its herbaceous
characteristics and often has grassy aromas. Other
flavors that come through include citrus, passion fruit,
fig, melon and even banana. Great food pairings
include any type of seafood, chicken, pork, goat cheese,
salads and dishes containing red peppers.*

# Creamy White / Cheese Sauce

1½ cups milk

¼ cup butter

3 Tbsp all-purpose flour

½ cup white wine

dash cayenne pepper

salt to taste

¾ cup grated cheddar cheese
(optional)

*This easy-to-prepare white/cheese sauce enhances fish, poultry and gratin dishes and can be used as the basis of many other sauces. If the milk is hot when you add it to the flour and butter mixture, there should not be any lumps. But if lumps do form, just put it into a blender for a few seconds.*

1. Bring the milk to a simmer in a small saucepan.

2. In a separate saucepan melt the butter over medium heat. Add the flour, stirring until well combined.

3. Slowly add the hot milk to the flour/butter mixture, stirring constantly until the sauce thickens. Add the wine and continue to simmer and stir over low heat for about 10 minutes. Season with cayenne pepper and salt.

4. If you only want a white sauce, you're finished at this point. If you're making cheese sauce, add the grated cheese and stir well. Remove from the heat when all the cheese has melted into the sauce.

MAKES 2 CUPS

# Cabernet Béarnaise Sauce

*featuring* CABERNET SAUVIGNON

*The good folks at Arbutus winery adapted this from a recipe that appeared in* Sunset *magazine. To make it you need some pan drippings from roast meat, and it's a perfect accompaniment to their Arbutus Beef Wellington, page 92. It also goes well with chicken, fish, steak and sweetbreads.*

½ cup Cabernet Sauvignon

2 Tbsp finely chopped shallots

3 tsp chopped fresh tarragon

pan drippings mixed with
    ¼ cup water

¾ cup butter

3 egg yolks

2 Tbsp lemon juice

1. Mix the wine, shallots, tarragon and drippings in a frying pan. Bring to a boil over high heat, stirring constantly. Continue boiling for about 5 minutes or until the liquid is reduced to ¼ cup. Keep the liquid hot.

2. Melt the butter in a saucepan over low heat. Turn the heat to high and cook for about 5 minutes or until the foam just begins to turn brown.

3. Place the egg yolks in a blender and mix at a high speed. Add the hot wine mixture, then gradually add the hot butter. Stir in the lemon juice. Serve hot or at room temperature.

SERVES 4–8

# Glacier Peak Meat Lover's Marinade

*featuring* GLACIER PEAK CABERNET SAUVIGNON

½ cup Cabernet Sauvignon

½ cup salad oil

¼ cup Worcestershire sauce

½ cup lemon juice

1–2 Tbsp minced garlic

1–2 Tbsp dried mustard

salt and freshly ground black
   pepper to taste

*This full-bodied, well-balanced wine has a dark rich aroma
that suggests black cherries. It has been aged in the barrel for
two years and then in the bottle for another two years. It really
enriches this marinade. Enjoy!*

1. Mix all the ingredients together in a resealable plastic bag
   or a covered non-reactive dish.

2. Marinate the meat of your choice for a minimum of
   4 hours, turning occasionally.

MAKES 2 CUPS

## GLACIER PEAK WINERY

58575 State Route 20, Rockport
TEL: (360) 770-9811
FAX: (360) 757-9772
www.glacierpeakwinery.com
gpwinery@msn.com

WINE SHOP, TOURS AND TASTINGS
Tasting room open weekends,
holidays and by appointment.
May–Sep., 10 a.m.–5 p.m. Tours and
tour buses are welcome.

GETTING THERE
Take Exit 232 from I-5. Head east
on Cook Road and then continue
heading east on Highway 20 and
drive right through Rockport. The
winery is located across from mile
post 104.

WINERY HIGHLIGHTS
Varietals grown at the vineyard are
Pinot Noir, Agria and Siegerrebe, a
light refreshing white wine. They also
bottle Cabernet Sauvignon, Merlot
and Syrah.

# Fox Estate Mystic Marinade

*featuring* FOX ESTATE MYSTIC GOLD

1 cup apple wine

½ cup peach or mango salsa
  (or any type of sweet, spicy
  salsa)

2 Tbsp teriyaki sauce

1 tsp Dijon mustard

¼ cup orange juice

1 tsp lime juice

1 clove garlic, crushed

*This marinade makes enough for 4 chicken breasts or about 1 lb of any mild white fish fillets. Mystic Gold is a true apple wine that has been blended with peach, and it appeals to the wine consumer as well the non-wine drinker. It goes well with spicy foods, such as Mexican, Chinese or Thai, and you can serve it chilled or warm with a cinnamon stick.*

*1.* This is just about the easiest recipe you will ever find. Combine all the ingredients in a large resealable bag or a non-reactive covered dish. Add the poultry or fish you want, cover and refrigerate.

*2.* Poultry should marinate for 12 hours and fish for up to 6 hours. Remember to turn it at least once. Enjoy your feast with a glass of Fox Estate Mystic Gold.

MAKES 2 CUPS

**FOX ESTATE WINERY**
24962 Highway 243 S, Mattawa
TEL: (509) 932-5818
www.foxestatewinery.com
support@foxestatewinery.com

WINE SHOP, TOURS AND TASTINGS
Open Mon.–Fri. 10 a.m.–5 p.m., on
weekends during the summer and
holidays, from noon–4 p.m.

GETTING THERE
Located just off Highway 243 South
on the east side of the Columbia
River 20 miles south of the Gorge
Amphitheater.

WINERY HIGHLIGHTS
The Fox Estate Riesling was voted
"Outstanding" in *Northwest Wine
Press* magazine.

# Dunham Cellars Sweet Onion Compote

*featuring* DUNHAM CELLARS SHIRLEY MAYS SEMILLON

½ cup olive oil

1 head elephant garlic, cloves
   separated, peeled and
   roughly chopped

4 large sweet onions (Walla
   Walla), roughly chopped

1 Tbsp turmeric

1 tsp nutmeg

½ cup honey

1 bottle Semillon

*This recipe uses the famous Walla Walla onions. The wine is a tribute to winemaker Eric Dunham's grandmother, Shirley Mays, a long-time resident of Walla Walla who died of breast cancer in 1983. A portion of the proceeds from the sale of this wine is donated to the Susan G. Komen Breast Cancer Foundation to help fund the fight against breast cancer.*

1. Heat the oil in a large frying pan over medium heat. Add the garlic and onions and cook until the onions begin to soften and caramelize, around 5 minutes. Add the turmeric, nutmeg and honey and stir until well combined. Stir in the wine.

2. Simmer uncovered over medium heat for up to 2 hours. When the liquid is cooked off, the onion compote will achieve a pasty consistency. Serve warm with steak.

SERVES 6–8

**DUNHAM CELLARS**
150 East Boeing Avenue, Walla Walla
TEL: (509) 529-4685
FAX: (509) 529-0201
www.dunhamcellars.com
wine@dunhamcellars.com

WINE SHOP, TOURS AND TASTINGS
Tasting room open daily
11 a.m.–4 p.m.

GETTING THERE
Head east on Highway 12 past
downtown Walla Walla. Take the
airport exit and turn left at the
stop sign. Travel under the highway
overpass and go about ⅓ mile past
the airport terminal. Turn right onto
Boeing Avenue.

WINERY HIGHLIGHTS
The winery makes its home in a
rustic, remodeled, World War II–era
airplane hangar.

# Pasek Cellars Blackberry Wine Balsamic Sauce for Salmon

*featuring* PASEK CELLARS BLACKBERRY WINE

**1 Tbsp butter**

**1 small onion, minced**

**1 clove garlic, diced**

**1 Tbsp chopped fresh rosemary**

**1 cup balsamic vinegar**

**2 cups blackberry wine**

*Savory Table Catering used Pasek's sweet, full-bodied blackberry wine to create this incredible sauce for salmon. The wine is available at retail locations in Washington and Oregon or at the Pasek Cellars tasting room. There is nothing better on salmon than this sauce. Try it once and you will be converted for life!*

*1.* Melt the butter in a saucepan over medium-high heat and sauté the onion and garlic until the onion is translucent and slightly browned, about 5 minutes.

*2.* Add the rosemary, balsamic vinegar and wine, and simmer on medium heat, stirring often. Simmer until the sauce has reduced by ⅔, leaving approximately 1 cup.

*3.* Pour the sauce over cooked salmon for a simple gourmet treat.

MAKES 1 CUP

## PASEK CELLARS WINERY TASTING ROOM

18729 Fir Island Road
(Skagit Red Barn), Conway
TEL: 1 (888) 350-9463
FAX: (360) 336-6877
www.pasekcellars.com
pasekwinery@hotmail.com

WINE SHOP, TOURS AND TASTINGS
Free wine tasting daily 11 a.m.–
5 p.m. Tasting also available at the
Masterpiece Gallery in Leavenworth.

GETTING THERE
The Conway Skagit Red Barn is just
south of Mount Vernon. It is just
west of I-5 exit 221. For Leavenworth
tastings, go to the 2nd floor of the
Masterpiece Gallery at 939 Front
Street.

WINERY HIGHLIGHTS
Pasek Cellars is the official wine
supplier for the Skagit Valley
Tulip Festival.

# Red Honey Mustard Marinade

**1 cup red wine**

**2 Tbsp Dijon mustard**

**½ cup olive oil**

**2 Tbsp honey**

**2 cloves garlic, crushed**

**2 Tbsp chopped fresh tarragon**

*Honey mustard is a universally popular marinade. This version features red wine and is great for lamb or beef. Try using different herbs, such as rosemary, dill or basil to change the flavor.*

1. Combine the ingredients in a saucepan and bring to a boil. Reduce the heat and simmer for 5 minutes, stirring occasionally. Refrigerate the marinade until cool before adding the meat.

2. Place the meat in a non-reactive covered container or resealable plastic bag and refrigerate for at least 3 and up to 24 hours, turning frequently.

MAKES 1½ CUPS

Silver Lake's Vineyard at Roza Hills in Zillah  (page 111)  PHOTO COURTESY OF SILVER LAKE WINERY

OPPOSITE:  Maryhill's Mouth-Watering Roast Game Hens  (page 84)

PREVIOUS PAGE:  Classic Belgian-Style Mussels  (page 62)

The beautifully landscaped backyard at Basel Cellars is the perfect venue for pool parties  (page 137)

The Desert Wind Vineyard (page 205) PHOTO COURTESY OF DESERT WIND WINERY

The view of Mount Hood from Wind River Cellars is spectacular (page 185) PHOTO COURTESY OF WIND RIVER CELLARS

OPPOSITE: Barnard Griffin Beef with Shallots, Pancetta and Port (page 120)

NEXT PAGE: Hedges Family Estate Fortified Poached Pears (page 168)

# Teriyaki Marinade

Teriyaki derives from teri, which means "shine" or "gloss" and yaki, which refers to cooked meat. Traditionally this recipe contains rice wine but we have adapted it and we're sure you'll agree the results are fabulous. Marinated meat can be pan-fried or cooked on the grill. This is great for kebabs, steaks, chicken, salmon and even prawns. This makes enough to cover 12 large kebabs, 8–10 chicken breasts or 2 lb of seafood.

¾ cup red wine
2 Tbsp olive oil
1½ cups soy sauce
1 clove garlic, crushed
½ cup brown sugar
1 tsp sesame oil
1-inch piece ginger, grated

1. Combine all the ingredients in a resealable plastic bag or non-reactive dish.

2. Cover and marinate your choice of meat, fish or seafood. Beef should be marinated overnight, chicken 2–3 hours, fish for about 30 minutes and prawns for 15 minutes.

MAKES 3 CUPS

# Reininger's Blueberry Merlot Barbecue Sauce

*featuring* REININGER MERLOT WALLA WALLA VALLEY

1 Tbsp extra virgin olive oil

½ onion, diced

1 clove garlic, minced

1 cup tomato sauce

1 cup Merlot

2 Tbsp balsamic vinegar

1 Tbsp brown sugar

1 cup blueberries
   (fresh or frozen)

*Believe us, this sauce will bring some excitement to your table. The Reininger Merlot is made with Walla Walla Valley fruit exclusively. It combines flavors of velvety currant, cocoa-espresso and exotic brown spice with aromas of dried cherry and rose. Blended with Cabernet Sauvignon and Cabernet Franc, it reflects classic Bordeaux.*

1. Heat the oil in a heavy saucepan over medium-high heat and sauté the onion and garlic until translucent, about 5 minutes. Add the tomato sauce, wine, vinegar and brown sugar and cook for about 2 minutes. Add the blueberries and cook until they burst, stirring occasionally.

2. Remove the pan from the heat. Using a hand-held blender, purée the sauce until smooth. Serve this sauce with chicken, ribs or any grilled meats.

MAKES 3–4 CUPS

**REININGER WINERY**
5858 West Highway 12, Walla Walla
TEL: (509) 522-1994
FAX: (509) 522-3530
www.reiningerwinery.com
info@reiningerwinery.com

WINE SHOP, TOURS AND TASTINGS
Open daily for tasting 10 a.m.–6 p.m.
Winter hours 10 a.m.–5 p.m. No
tasting fee (with the exception of $5
per person for parties of 20 or more).
Tours available by appointment only.

GETTING THERE
Located on Highway 12 just 6 miles
west of Walla Walla.

WINERY HIGHLIGHTS
This was the first winery to expressly
concentrate on Walla Walla Valley
fruit. Chuck Reininger's background
as a mountain climbing guide and
outdoor adventurer has shaped his
philosophy about the land and about
winemaking.

# Merlot

*pronounced (*MARE-LOW*)*

*Historians have traced Merlot as far back as first-century France. Merlot is one of the acclaimed red varieties of Bordeaux, where it became famous during the 1800s. This wine is usually a little softer and perhaps warmer than Cabernet Sauvignon.*

*The wine has been growing in popularity since the late 1970s, when winemakers in North America discovered that the grape is not only good for blending, but also produces wonderful wine on its own. Its popularity fell a little after the release of the film* **Sideways**; *however, we've been assured it's now rising once again, as it's the most popular red in the United States. This is good news, as Washington is recognized as producing some of the best Merlots in the world.*

*Merlot grapes mature earlier and are larger than Cabernet Sauvignon grapes. They also have a thicker skin. This wine is not great for long-term cellaring, unless it is blended. This probably accounts for some of its recent popularity, as many consumers prefer the convenience of having a great wine to drink immediately rather than waiting for the cellaring process.*

*Common characteristics displayed in Merlot include plum, blackcurrant, cherry, vanilla and cloves. The wine pairs well with lamb, grilled meats, wild game, hearty pastas, duck, chocolate and aged cheeses.*

# Three Rivers Bing Cherry Demi-Glace

*featuring* THREE RIVERS MERITAGE

¾ cup red wine

pinch kosher salt

½ tsp freshly ground pepper

1 bay leaf

1 oz dried sweet Bing cherries (available at health-food stores)

13 oz demi-glace or veal stock (available at specialty stores or online)

*Executive Chef Jamie Brandt, of Lake Crescent Lodge on the Olympic Peninsula, created and served this demi-glace with rack of lamb at a local winemakers' dinner, and it was a big hit. This Meritage is a beautiful example of how complex and harmonious Bordeaux grape varietals can be when blended together. It has tremendous aging potential and will be drinkable well into the future. The grapes are hand-picked from the best of the Columbia Valley vineyards; initial fermentation on the skins and secondary malolactic fermentation in small French oak barrels adds a nice depth and complexity to the wine. Leftover sauce can be frozen in a sealed plastic container.*

*1.* Add the red wine to a saucepan over high heat. Add the salt, pepper and bay leaves. Reduce by ¼, then add the cherries and reduce by another ¼ so that only half the original amount remains.

*2.* Reduce the heat to medium, add the demi-glace or stock and mix well. Let it reduce by ¼ or until the sauce is just thick enough to coat a spoon. Do not make it as thick as your grandma's gravy!

*3.* You should be able to taste all of the flavors—just enough salt, a little peppery, sweet cherry and not too overpowering on the wine taste. Serve it with any red meat, game or pork. Recommended over roasted rack of lamb.

SERVES 8

## THREE RIVERS WINERY

5641 West Highway 12, Walla Walla
TEL: (509) 526-9463
FAX: (509) 529-3436
www.threeriverswinery.com
info@threeriverswinery.com

### WINE SHOP, TOURS AND TASTINGS

Open daily 10 a.m.–6 p.m. except
Christmas, Thanksgiving and
New Year's Day. They have a
complimentary and reserve wine
tasting list and a well-stocked gift
shop. Tours available upon request.

### GETTING THERE

The winery is located 6 miles west of
Walla Walla on Highway 12.

### WINERY HIGHLIGHTS

Try your luck on the 3-hole golf
course or come for a picnic on
the deck with a view of the Blue
Mountains. You might even meet
winemaker Holly Turner, who
continues to garner awards and
attention from the press for her gold
medal wines.

### WINERY SPECIAL OFFER

Show your copy of this book and
receive a free reserve wine tasting
valued at $5.

# Desserts

If a life of wine, women and song
becomes too much . . . give up the singing!

*—Anonymous*

# Hedges Family Estate Fortified Poached Pears

*featuring* HEDGES FAMILY ESTATE RED MOUNTAIN FORTIFIED AND THREE VINEYARDS

6 Bosc pears, peeled, halved
  and cored

3 cups red wine

1½ cups fortified port-style
  dessert wine

½ cup sugar

2 Tbsp lemon juice

¼ cup orange juice

2 Tbsp chopped lemon zest

4 Tbsp chopped orange zest

1 cinnamon stick (2 inches)

vanilla ice cream

fresh mint and shortbread
  cookies for garnish

*This recipe showcases two of Hedges Estate's most popular wines. Three Vineyards is the flagship of their estate wines, a blend of fruit from their three vineyards: Hedges Estate, Bel'Villa and Red Mountain. Red Mountain Fortified is a port-style dessert wine blended from the traditional Portuguese varietals Tinta Cão, Touriga and Souzao and fortified with brandy. Never cloying or overly sweet, Red Mountain Fortified provides enough sweetness to accompany a dessert, but retains structure, complexity and balance.*

1. Place the pear halves in a single layer in a wide pan, flat side down. Add the red wine, dessert wine, sugar, juice, zest and cinnamon stick. Bring to a boil over high heat. Reduce the heat and simmer uncovered until the pears are tender, 10–15 minutes for ripe pears. (Underripe pears may not achieve tenderness for 20–25 minutes.)

2. Remove the pears to a bowl and strain the poaching liquid over them. Refrigerate for 2 hours or overnight. (The recipe can be prepared to this point up to 2 days in advance.)

3. To serve, place a scoop of vanilla ice cream in the bottom of a dessert bowl. Place 2 pear halves to the side of the ice cream and pour some poaching liquid overtop. Garnish with a shortbread cookie and a sprig of mint.

SERVES 6

## HEDGES FAMILY ESTATE ON RED MOUNTAIN

53511 North Sunset Road
Benton City
TEL: (509) 588-3155
FAX: (509) 588-5323
www.hedgesfamilyestate.com
hedgescellarswinery@msn.com

### WINE SHOP, TOURS AND TASTINGS

Visitors are welcome Mar.–Dec., Fri.–Sun. 11 a.m.–5 p.m. A small tasting fee is refunded upon purchase.

### GETTING THERE

From Seattle take I-90 eastbound. Directly after Ellensburg take exit 110, I-82 eastbound, through Yakima/Tri Cities. Take exit 96 off I-82. At the end of the off ramp, take a left under the freeway. Take the first right onto Highway 224 toward West Richland. Follow Highway 224 for 1½ miles, turn left onto Sunset Road and follow for 2 miles. Hedges Family Estate is on the right.

### WINERY HIGHLIGHTS

A large stone fireplace, 14-foot ceilings and a beautiful handcrafted wood bar make the tasting room an experience to remember. Old-world European style melds with modern winemaking technology at this winery. It is surrounded by a beautiful courtyard garden that boasts a stunning view of the Red Mountain AVA.

# Cheesecake with Raspberry Wine Sauce

*featuring* RASPBERRY WINE

2 cups graham cracker crumbs

1½ cups sugar

¼ cup melted butter

1 tsp ground cinnamon

2 packages cream cheese
(8 oz each)

1 tsp vanilla essence

¼ tsp almond extract

4 eggs

3 cups sour cream

1½ cups raspberry wine

1 tsp unflavored gelatin (or 1
packet Oetker clear glaze)

*This recipe came to us from the Hoodsport Winery and was inspired by their delicious raspberry wine. For a different topping, experiment with other fruit wines.*

1. Preheat the oven to 350°F. Combine the cracker crumbs, ¼ cup of the sugar, melted margarine and cinnamon in a bowl and mix well. Press the mixture into the base of a 9- or 10-inch springform pan.

2. Put the cream cheese in a separate large bowl and add the remaining 1¼ cups of sugar, vanilla and almond extract. Add the eggs 1 at a time, mixing each in well. Stir in the sour cream in batches, mixing well before you add the next batch. It should not get too thin too quickly.

3. Pour the mixture over the graham cracker crust. Bake for about 50 minutes. It will not get brown on top so to test if it is done rub your finger gently on top. If the film on the surface crinkles it is not done. It should not pull away and it should not be sticky. Refrigerate the cheesecake until thoroughly chilled.

4. To make the topping, heat the wine and dissolve the gelatin in it. (If using the glaze packet, follow glaze directions but replace the liquid with wine.) Chill the mixture until it is the consistency of egg whites. Pour the chilled topping over the chilled cheesecake and spread evenly. Chill again. Serve with a glass of raspberry wine.

SERVES 8

# Fourth of July Fruit Salad

*This red, white and blue fruit salad is a visual treat for a July Fourth barbecue or picnic, and it tastes fantastic! Adjust the sugar level if you have a sweet white wine, as the recipe was created with a dry white wine in mind.*

1 cup dry white wine

¼ cup sugar

1 cup blueberries

4 cups strawberries, halved

2 red apples, cored and chopped

1. Combine the wine and sugar in a small saucepan. Bring to a boil and stir until the sugar dissolves. Simmer for 2 minutes before removing from the heat.

2. Combine the fruit in a bowl and pour the warm wine mixture overtop. Mix thoroughly, cover and refrigerate until chilled.

SERVES 4

# La Toscana's Famous Grape Cake

*featuring* La Toscana Late Harvest Gewürztraminer

1½ cups all-purpose flour

1 tsp baking powder

1 tsp salt

¼ tsp baking soda

¾ cup + 3 Tbsp sugar

8 Tbsp softened unsalted butter

3 Tbsp extra virgin olive oil

2 large eggs, beaten

1 tsp grated lemon zest

1 tsp grated orange zest

1 tsp vanilla essence

1 cup late harvest Gewürztraminer

1½ cups small red seedless grapes

*The late-harvest Gewürztraminer used in this recipe is fruity, sweet and aromatic, with a smooth finish. This elegant wine is a treat with fruit or as an after-dinner specialty, and it brings a marvelous mix of sweetness and spice to the cake. This is a dessert your family will ask for again and again.*

*1.* Preheat the oven to 400°F. Brush a 10-inch springform pan with olive oil. Line the bottom with parchment paper and brush the paper with olive oil.

*2.* Sift the flour, baking powder, salt and baking soda into a large bowl. Combine the ¾ cup of sugar, 6 Tbsp of the butter and the olive oil in a separate bowl and whisk until smooth. Whisk in the beaten eggs, orange and lemon zest and vanilla. Add the flour mixture alternately with the wine in 3 additions, whisking smooth after each addition.

*3.* Transfer the batter to the prepared pan and smooth the top. Sprinkle the grapes over the batter and bake the cake until the top is set, about 20 minutes. Dot the top of the cake with the remaining 2 Tbsp of butter and sprinkle with the remaining 3 Tbsp of sugar. Bake until golden and an inserted tester comes out clean, about 20 minutes more.

*4.* Cool in the pan on a rack for 20 minutes, then release the pan sides. Serve it slightly warm. This cake is divine with a dab of mascarpone and a drizzle of vin santo.

Serves 6–8

**LA TOSCANA WINERY**
9020 Foster Road, Cashmere
TEL: (509) 548-5448
www.latoscanawinery.com
wmoyles@nwi.net

WINE SHOP, TOURS AND TASTINGS
Tasting room open by appointment
only. Just call ahead.

GETTING THERE
As you head into Cashmere from the
west on Highway 2 or 97 you will see
Foster Road on your left. It is after
the Big Y Café and just before the
Shell station. The winery is located a
little way down, on the left.

WINERY HIGHLIGHTS
During summer you can taste
outdoors under a lush arbor of
grapevines adjacent to the winery.
Combine a wine tasting with a stay
in La Toscana's bed and breakfast.
The luxurious room is made for a
romantic getaway in any season.

# Marchetti Wines Biscotti à la Emma

*featuring* MARCHETTI OLD VINE ZINFANDEL

1½ cups sugar

½ cup butter

4 eggs

2 tsp vanilla extract

1 tsp lemon extract

1 tsp almond extract

1–3 tsp anise extract

¾ cup milk

4–5 cups all-purpose flour

1 cup sliced almonds

*Biscotti, Italian biscuits traditionally dunked in red wine, are also great with dessert wine or coffee. We recommend dunking these biscotti in Marchetti Old Vine Zinfandel. "Old vine" means the grapevines are at least 50 years old. The wine is dark, rich and full bodied, with lots of velvety fruit flavors. It is racy, audacious, loud and chewy to the point of almost needing a knife and fork!*

*1.* Preheat the oven to 350°F. Cream the sugar and butter together in a large bowl. Add the eggs, vanilla, lemon, almond and anise extracts, milk and flour. Mix it all together by hand until it has the consistency of cookie dough. Add the sliced almonds and mix them through.

*2.* Roll out the dough into 2 logs, each about 1 inch wide and 12 inches long. Place on a greased cookie sheet and bake in the middle of the oven for 25 minutes, until golden brown.

*3.* After baking, turn the biscotti upside down and let them cool. Slice diagonally, pour a glass of Zinfandel and enjoy your biscotti dunked in wine.

SERVES 10

MARCHETTI WINES

3709 Fuller Lane SE, Olympia

TEL: (360) 438-8851

www.marchettiwines.com

rich@marchettiwines.com

WINE SHOP, TOURS AND TASTINGS
Unfortunately, due to local zoning
laws, tours and tastings are not
offered at this winery.

WINERY HIGHLIGHTS
Marchetti wines are made in the
old-world tradition without any
chemicals or preservatives. A process
of natural fermentation is used and
the flavors are purely from the grapes
themselves and the oak barrels in
which the wine is aged.

# Zinfandel

*pronounced (ZIN-FAN-DEL)*

*Zinfandel has been grown in the United States for a long time. It is thought it was first introduced during the early 1800s. By the latter half of that century the wine was being produced in fairly large quantities in California, as the hardy grapes survived with minimal attention. Recent DNA technology has proved that Zinfandel is actually the same as the grape known as Primitivo in Italy.*

*It was not until the late 1980s and early 1990s that the grape really began to take off in the USA, first as a light pink, sweeter wine and later as a deep dark red. It is argued by some that the very best Zinfandel comes from 70-, 80-, even 100-year-old vines. Even with Washington's young vines some marvelous wine is being produced, and it is well worth trying.*

*Zinfandel is not recognized as a wine for cellaring and it is usually best consumed within 5 years of the vintage. An exception to this rule can be made with the heavier wine styles; however, the wine does lose its unique Zinfandel characteristics during prolonged bottle aging.*

*This is a versatile grape that results in diverse styles ranging from white Zinfandel (which is not a different variety of grape, just a different style of winemaking) through to heavy port-style wines.*

*Common characteristics of Washington Zinfandel include aromas of berry fruit, licorice, spice and black pepper and flavors of chocolate, black cherries, leather and spice. It pairs well with pizza, burgers, game and Stilton cheese and can usually hold up well to Asian cuisine.*

# Napeequa's Chocolate Shortbread and French Vanilla Ice Cream with Cherry Sauce

*featuring* NAPEEQUA GLISSADE

2 cups canned dark sweet cherries (or use a 16-oz can)

⅛ tsp ground cinnamon

¼ cup dessert wine

2 tsp cornstarch

1 cup unsalted butter

½ cup sugar

1 tsp vanilla extract

½ cup unsweetened cocoa powder

1¾ cups all-purpose flour

½ tsp kosher salt

2 quarts French vanilla ice cream (use store-bought or see the chef's tip, facing page, and make your own!)

semi-sweet chocolate shavings for garnish (optional)

*Napeequa Glissade is a dessert-style wine that begins with whole cluster pressings of Gewürztraminer grapes in subfreezing temperatures (fashioned after the great German Trockenbeerenauslese, or TBA). A three-hour press cycle tenderly extracts the honey-colored juice. After settling, the juice is inoculated with special European dessert wine yeast designed to enhance the natural Gewürztraminer aromatics and improve structure.*

*1.* Combine the juice from the cherries, cinnamon, wine and cornstarch in a small saucepan. Cook on medium-low heat, stirring constantly, until the sauce turns dark and thickens slightly. Remove from the heat and add the cherries. Let the sauce cool to room temperature, cover and set aside or refrigerate. (If refrigerated, heat sauce slightly before using.)

*2.* Preheat the oven to 325°F. Using an electric mixer with a paddle attachment, cream the butter and sugar together until light and fluffy. Stir in the vanilla.

*3.* Sift the cocoa, flour and salt together and add to the butter mixture. Mix just until everything is well combined. Remove the dough to a lightly floured surface. Flour the top of the dough lightly and use a floured rolling pin to roll the dough out to just less than ¼ inch thick. Do not roll the dough too thin! Cut the dough with a 4-inch round cookie cutter (or any other shape you like). Place the cookies about 1 inch apart on a parchment-lined baking sheet. Gather the dough scraps and roll again to make more cookies.

**NAPEEQUA VINTNERS INC**
8820 Beaver Valley Road
Leavenworth
Seattle office:
TEL: (206) 930-7501
FAX: (206) 323-7126
www.napeequa.com
michael@napeequa.com

WINE SHOP, TOURS AND TASTINGS
Tasting room open on holiday
weekends and by appointment.

GETTING THERE
From Seattle take I-5 north to Everett.
Turn right (east) onto Highway 2
toward Stevens Pass and Wenatchee.
Follow for 85 miles, then turn left
(north) on Highway 207 toward Lake
Wenatchee and follow for 8 miles.
Turn right (east) on Highway 209
toward Plain and follow for 5 miles
before turning right onto Beaver Valley
Road. The winery is on the right.

WINERY HIGHLIGHTS
This is one of the highest wineries, in
terms of elevation, in the Northwest.

**4.** Bake the cookies for 15 minutes or until they are firm
to the touch. Turn the pans around once or twice
during the cooking process. Allow the cookies to cool
before removing them from the parchment. To serve,
place a cookie on a dessert plate, top with a scoop of
ice cream and pour sauce overtop. Top with shavings
of semi-sweet chocolate, if using.

SERVES 8

CHEF'S TIP
*If you have an ice cream maker, it's simple to make
your own delicious French vanilla ice cream at home.
Combine 3 cups half-and-half cream with 1 cup sugar
and 4 beaten egg yolks in a medium saucepan over
low heat. Stir until the mixture coats the spoon and is
slightly thickened. Cool to room temperature, then stir
in 1 cup whipping cream and 1 Tbsp vanilla extract.
Pour into an ice cream maker and freeze according
to the manufacturer's directions. This makes about
2 quarts.*

# Strawberries and Mint

1 cup red wine

¼ cup sugar

2 Tbsp lemon juice

2 Tbsp chopped fresh mint

1 lb strawberries, green tops
removed

*Fresh berries are wonderful macerated in red wine, and the mint adds a refreshing note. Try substituting fresh basil for the mint. It sounds strange but it is just as good.*

*1.* Mix the wine, sugar, lemon juice and mint in a large bowl.

*2.* Add the strawberries and allow them to soak in the mixture for 2 hours.

*3.* Serve the berries on their own with whipped cream or ice cream. Pour a little of the wine sauce overtop.

SERVES 4–6

# Icewine

In the late 1700s winemakers in Franconia, Germany, were alarmed to find that an extreme cold spell had left their grapes frozen on the vines. They decided not to lose the harvest and went ahead pressing the juice from the frozen grapes. The results left them dumbfounded; they had just made the world's first icewine.

The grapes used to make real icewine must be hand-picked in extremely cold temperatures, usually between 17 and 9° Fahrenheit. When pressed in this state, because the water in the grape is still ice, only a few precious drops of extremely sweet, concentrated liquid can be extracted. This juice is allowed to settle before it is clarified and fermented.

It takes a lot more grapes to produce a 7-oz bottle of icewine than it does to produce a regular 26-oz bottle of wine. This is one of the reasons icewine is more expensive than other types of wine.

Washington is producing some truly magnificent examples of icewine, both red and white. Producers like Chateau Ste. Michelle, Covey Run and C. R. Sandidge have all produced award-winning icewines.

Icewine is always sweet, yet each grape variety retains its own characteristics. The wine should be served chilled, but not cold. The ideal temperature is believed to be between 50 and 54°F. Most icewines should be consumed while young, though notable exceptions are Riesling and Pinot Noir, which have proven to cellar well. Once opened, a bottle will last three to five days in the refrigerator, as long as it has been recorked.

# Page Cellars Syrah Chocolate Brownies

*featuring* PAGE CELLARS SYRAH

**12 oz semi-sweet or dark chocolate chips**

**3 Tbsp unsweetened cocoa**

**¾ cup butter**

**2 eggs plus 1 extra yolk**

**½ tsp salt**

**1 tsp vanilla extract**

**2¼ cups sugar**

**¼ cup Syrah**

**1½ cups all-purpose flour, sifted**

**1 cup chopped nuts (optional)**

*This gold medal winner is a fruit-forward wine showcasing raspberry, cherry and blackberry. It has generous aromatics and a lush velvety finish. It's delicious with glazed salmon or pork, with spicy entrées or all by itself! Of course, we also suggest drinking it with these marvelous brownies.*

*1.* Preheat the oven to 350°F. Melt half the chocolate chips with the cocoa and butter in a heavy saucepan or double boiler, stirring constantly. When all is melted and mixed, remove from the heat and allow to cool slightly.

*2.* Beat the eggs (including the extra yolk) and salt, gradually adding the vanilla, sugar and wine. Continue beating for 8–10 minutes.

*3.* Gently fold the chocolate mixture into the sugar and egg mixture. Then fold in the remaining chocolate chips, flour and nuts (if using). Make sure it is all thoroughly mixed together.

*4.* Pour the mixture into a well greased 13- × 9- × 2-inch pan. Bake for 25–30 minutes. Remove from the oven and cover with foil to keep it moist while cooling. Enjoy with a glass of Syrah.

SERVES 4

## PAGE CELLARS

19495 144th Avenue NW, Suite B235

Woodinville

TEL: (253) 232-9463

FAX: (253) 265-2875

www.pagecellars.com

page@earthlink.net

### WINE SHOP, TOURS AND TASTINGS

Open for tasting every Sat.

noon–4 p.m.

### GETTING THERE

From Seattle take I-90 or I-520 to the 405 northbound. Take exit 23 onto the 522 heading east, then exit at 195th Avenue NE and continue uphill before turning left on 144th Avenue NE.

### WINERY HIGHLIGHTS

This family-owned boutique winery produces upward of 1,500 cases of premium wine per year.

# Sky River Trifle

*featuring* SKY RIVER SWEET MEAD

1 cup half-and-half (or use
 ½ cup milk and ½ cup
 whipping cream)

3 egg yolks

2 Tbsp sugar

dash of salt

2 tsp cornstarch

½ cup sweet mead

1 package ladyfingers (12
 ladyfingers or 12 slices of
 sponge cake)

⅓ cup strawberry preserves

1 can pears or fruit cocktail
 (15 oz), well drained

1 cup whipping cream

2 Tbsp honey

cherries or slivered almonds
 for garnish

*The floral notes and lingering honey taste of Sky River Sweet Mead give this trifle a lovely boost. Enjoy the mead as a delicate aperitif or dessert wine. It is a genuine indulgence served warm with a touch of cinnamon or cardamom or chilled with a splash of ginger ale.*

1. Scald the half-and-half in a heavy saucepan over low heat. Stir occasionally until it begins to steam and small bubbles appear around the edges of the saucepan. Do not boil. Remove from the heat and set aside to cool slightly.

2. Whisk the egg yolks in a bowl and then slowly add the sugar, salt, cornstarch and scalded cream. Microwave the mixture on high for 1–2 minutes until thickened. Stir in 2 Tbsp of the mead and place in the refrigerator to chill.

3. Split the ladyfingers. Spread with strawberry preserves, then sandwich them back together. Cube the ladyfinger sandwiches and place them in a flat-bottomed glass bowl. Cover with the fruit, then drizzle with the remaining mead.

4. Cover the fruit with the custard sauce. Place in the refrigerator to chill.

5. Just before serving the trifle, whip the whipping cream and honey in a bowl until stiff peaks form. Top the trifle with whipped cream and garnish with cherries or almonds.

SERVES 4–6

**SKY RIVER MEADERY**

32533 Cascade View Drive, Sultan

TEL: (360) 793-6761

FAX: (360) 793-2485

www.skyriverbrewing.com

info@skyriverbrewing.com

WINE SHOP, TOURS AND TASTINGS

Tasting and tours available Mon.-Fri.
10 a.m.-4 p.m.

GETTING THERE

Follow Highway 2 east to Sultan.
Turn right on Cascade View Drive,
east of town. Signs will direct you to
the meadery.

WINERY HIGHLIGHTS

View the stunning landscape at the
foothills of the Columbia Mountains
and see first-hand how Sky River has
introduced mead to the 21st century.

# Mead

*pronounced (MEED)*

*Mead has been around for a very long time. Legend has it that old King Midas was a mead drinker; and Norse gods were also fond of imbibing the intoxicating nectar in Valhalla. Today, perhaps aided by movies such as* **The Lord of the Rings***, mead is experiencing a resurgence.*

*Mead is a fermented alcoholic beverage made of honey, water and yeast. If you've never tried mead (and most people haven't), it's well worth a trip to one of the meaderies to sample some; otherwise look for it in your local wine stores or supermarkets. If they don't sell it, ask them to get some in for you. Washington producers include Sky River Mead and Olympic Cellars.*

*Mead can be paired successfully with many types of foods, but with so many types of mead (ranging from sweet through to dry) it is difficult to generalize. Some of the meads we've tried paired well with spicy dishes, shellfish and Asian cuisine. Mead also goes well with dessert, and some varieties are sweet enough to be consumed as a dessert on their own.*

# Wind River Cellars Raspberry Chocolate Truffle Cake

*featuring* WIND RIVER PORT OF CELIO

**17 oz bittersweet chocolate**

**¾ cup unsalted butter**

**⅔ cup sugar**

**5 large eggs**

**6 Tbsp all-purpose flour**

**¼ cup whipping cream**

**¼ cup brewed espresso**

**1 Tbsp port**

**3 half-pints fresh raspberries**

*Made from the traditional Portuguese method, this dessert wine has created a buzz in the Northwest. Distilled grape brandy infused into fermenting red wine produces a thick, flavorful port with loads of marionberry, blackberry and chocolate.*

*1.* Preheat the oven to 350°F and butter a 10-inch springform pan. Chop 10½ oz of the chocolate and just over ½ cup of the butter into pieces. Melt the chopped chocolate and butter with the sugar in a double boiler or a metal bowl set over a saucepan of barely simmering water, stirring until smooth (the sugar will not be dissolved). Remove from the heat and cool to room temperature. Transfer the mixture to a large bowl.

*2.* Separate the eggs, putting the yolks in a small bowl and the whites in a large bowl. Add the yolks 1 at a time to the chocolate mixture, whisking after each addition. Beat the egg whites until they just hold soft peaks. Sift the flour over the chocolate mixture. Use a whisk to gently but thoroughly fold the flour and half the egg whites into the mixture. Use a rubber spatula to gently fold in the remaining whites.

*3.* Pour the batter into the pan, smoothing the top. Bake in the middle of the oven for 40–45 minutes or until a tester inserted in the center comes out clean. Cool the cake in the pan on a rack.

**WIND RIVER CELLARS**
196 Spring Creek Road, Husum
TEL: (509) 493-2324
www.windrivercellars.com
info@windrivercellars.com

WINE SHOP, TOURS AND TASTINGS
Open daily 10 a.m.–6 p.m. Closed
Dec. 15–Jan. 1. The $5 tasting fee is
waived if you purchase wine.

GETTING THERE
Located 8 miles north of Hood River,
Oregon, on the Washington side.
Take Highway 141 north toward Mt.
Adams. From Husum, follow signs to
the winery.

WINERY HIGHLIGHTS
Taste the largest variety of wines
in the Columbia River Gorge. Take
advantage of whitewater rafting and
wine trips on the White Salmon River
from April to October.

WINERY SPECIAL OFFER
Show this book and receive 5 percent
discount in the tasting room.

4. To make the ganache, chop the remaining 6½ oz of chocolate and melt in the double boiler as in step 1. Stir until smooth, then remove from the heat. While the chocolate is melting bring the cream to a simmer in a small saucepan and add the espresso. Add the cream mix, the remaining butter and the port to the chocolate and stir until smooth.

5. Remove the side of the pan and cut the cake into 8 wedges. Place the wedges on a large rack set over a large shallow baking pan, spacing them at least 1 inch apart. Pour enough warm ganache evenly over the wedges to coat them and let stand 5 minutes.

6. Scrape the excess ganache from the baking pan into the bowl of ganache and pour the ganache over the wedges again, making sure they are coated completely. (The remaining ganache may be kept and reheated as chocolate sauce.) Let the wedges stand until the ganache is set, at least 1 hour and up to 6. Just before serving cover the top of each wedge with fresh raspberries.

SERVES 12

# Drinks

My only regret in life is that
I did not drink more champagne.

—*John Maynard Keynes's dying words*

# Columbia Winery Pinot Gris Spritzer

*featuring* COLUMBIA PINOT GRIS

**1 slice lemon**

**1 slice lime**

**⅔ glass Pinot Gris**

**⅓ glass sparkling water**

*Refreshing spritzers are at home on the patio at a family barbecue. The Columbia Pinot Gris is full and fresh, with flavors of peach and melon followed by a lively finish. It's great on its own and equally delicious in this simple spritzer.*

1. Fill a large wineglass with ice. Squeeze the lemon and lime slices over the ice and then slide them down the side of the glass between the ice and the glass.

2. Pour in the Pinot Gris and top with the sparkling water. Stir with a cocktail stick or straw.

3. Enjoy your refreshing beverage outside in the sun and, perhaps, follow it with another one.

SERVES 1

**COLUMBIA WINERY**
14030 NE 145th, Woodinville
TEL: (425) 488-2776
www.columbiawinery.com
contact@columbiawinery.com

WINE SHOP, TOURS AND TASTINGS
Open daily 10 a.m.-7 p.m. (closes at
5 p.m. Oct.-Feb.)

GETTING THERE
Proceed north on I-405 to the
Monroe/Wenatchee exit (Highway
522). Follow Highway 522 to the first
Woodinville exit (sign for SR202).
Turn right and follow 132nd Avenue
NE to the second light (NE 175th
Street). Turn right on NE 175th
Street and continue to Highway
202 (approximately ½ mile). Turn
left on Highway 202 and continue
approximately 2 miles. Columbia
Winery is on the left as Highway 202
turns into NE 145th.

WINERY HIGHLIGHTS
Sample the wares at the largest wine-
tasting bar in Washington State!

# Pinot Gris

*pronounced (PEE-NO-GREE)*

*Pinot Gris is a mutation of the Pinot Noir grape. It is known as Pinot Grigio in Italy, Tokay d'Alsace in France and Grauburgunder or Rülander in Germany. Originally from Burgundy, it has been around since the Middle Ages.* **Gris** *means "gray" in French and refers to the color often found in the grapes, although in Washington they are commonly more of a pinkish brown. The Washington climate is perfect for the grape and the natural acidity in the soil produces clean, fresh flavors in the wine. In hotter climates the grape does not do as well.*

*Pinot Gris can be tangy and light or rich and full-bodied, depending on the ripeness of the grapes and the techniques used to create the wine. The wine is full of lively flavors and generally contains aromas of fresh fruits, such as pear, melon and apple.*

*Although Pinot Gris is not grown as widely in Washington as it is in Oregon, some excellent Pinot Gris is being produced in this state, albeit in small quantities. This varietal will continue to rise in popularity, as it makes an excellent accompaniment to westcoast seafood. It also pairs well with sushi and holds up against strong cheeses, such as brie and even Stilton.*

# Simple Sangria

1 bottle red wine

1 cup orange juice

1 orange, peeled and chopped

4 peaches, chopped

3 Tbsp sugar

*There must be a million recipes for sangria, but the best part of making this drink is that you can use whatever fruits, juices, wine or even hard liquor you have handy at the time. Try this version and feel free to experiment. You can use whatever fruits are in season, including apples, kiwis, pears, mandarins, pineapple and melon. If you want a bit more kick, try adding some vodka or rum. In this recipe about ½ cup should do the job nicely.*

*1.* Mix all the ingredients together in a large pitcher.

*2.* Put the pitcher in the fridge and let it sit for 3–4 hours before serving. This allows the fruit to absorb the wine and the wine to be flavored by the fruit.

*3.* Serve over ice.

SERVES 4

# Grape Vine

*featuring* ROSÉ

This cocktail comes courtesy of Gavin Forbes, the famous mixologist and the founder of Company Bar in the United Kingdom. This wine and gin concoction looks great and is guaranteed to delight.

1 oz gin (preferably Bombay Sapphire)

½ oz elderflower cordial (available at specialty food stores)

2 oz rosé wine

½ oz fresh lemon juice

5 red grapes

1 tsp sugar

*1.* Combine all the ingredients in a cocktail shaker and muddle them together (crush all the ingredients together using a wooden muddler or the back of a spoon). Add ice and shake well before straining into a martini glass. Serve with extra grapes or a flower to garnish.

SERVES 1

## BARTENDER'S TIP

*If you can't find elderflower cordial, you can try making something similar using elderflower tea. Just make 1 cup of strong elderflower tea, add 1 cup of white sugar and 2 cups of boiling water. Combine in a heatproof mixing jug and stir until the sugar has dissolved. The liquid should be thick and syrupy. When it has cooled, transfer to a bottle and keep in the refrigerator. You can make other flavors of bar syrup by using different teas, such as lavender or fruit teas. In no time you'll be inventing classy cocktails with these awesome bar syrups!*

# Hogue's Mulled Merlot

*featuring* MERLOT

2 oranges, sliced

1 lemon, sliced

1 bottle Merlot

¼ cup brandy

10 cloves

½ cup honey

7 cinnamon sticks

*Mulled wine, a treat at Christmas or during the winter months, is at its best when made with a full-flavored Merlot. Hogue Merlot, produced from the outstanding fruit of the Columbia Valley, is bursting with cranberry and black cherry flavors.*

*1.* Combine all the ingredients in a saucepan, reserving 4 cinnamon sticks for garnish. Heat slowly. Remember the saying for mulled wine: "If it boils, it spoils."

*2.* Stir to be sure the honey dissolves completely. When it is hot and delicious, about 20 minutes later, taste to make sure you are satisfied. If you want it sweeter, you can add more honey.

*3.* Pour into mugs and serve with the remaining 4 cinnamon sticks.

SERVES 4

## HOGUE CELLARS

2880 Lee Road, Prosser
TEL: (509) 786-4557 or
1 (800) 565-9779
FAX: (509) 786-4580
www.hoguecellars.com
info@hoguecellars.com

WINE SHOP, TOURS AND TASTINGS
Open daily 10 a.m.–5 p.m. except
major holidays. Hours may change
during winter, so please call ahead.

GETTING THERE
From Seattle take I-90 east toward
Spokane. Merge onto I-82 E via exit
110 toward Yakima. Head east on
Wine Country Road, then turn left
onto Benitz Road. Turn right onto
Lee Road.

WINERY HIGHLIGHTS
Hogue wines are often featured in
*Wine Spectator*'s Top 100 Wines of
the Year list.

# Mountain Dome Magic Cocktail

*featuring* MOUNTAIN DOME NON VINTAGE BRUT

1 cube sugar

1 drop Angostura bitters

1 tsp Grand Marnier
 (or Triple Sec)

1 tsp brandy

1 glass sparkling wine

1 orange peel twist

*Michael Manz, the winemaker at Mountain Dome Winery, has adapted a classic champagne cocktail to make a drink that will bring a touch of class to any occasion. If you're hosting a large function, you can have the glasses ready to go except for the bubbles.*

1. Place the sugar cube in the bottom of a champagne flute. Place a tiny drop of Angostura bitters onto the sugar. Add the Grand Marnier and brandy and top with sparkling wine.

2. Drop in twist of orange peel and you're ready to enjoy the bubbles.

SERVES 1

## MOUNTAIN DOME WINERY

16315 East Temple Road, Spokane

TEL: (509) 928-2788

FAX: (509) 922-8078

www.mountaindome.com

manz@mountaindome.com

WINE SHOP, TOURS AND TASTINGS
Open Sat. 11 a.m.–5 p.m. during
summer and by appointment
year-round.

GETTING THERE
Just 30 minutes NE of downtown
Spokane the winery is off Forker
Road.

WINERY HIGHLIGHTS
Visit the smiling gnomes and the
marvelous 4,000-square-foot
geodesic dome home. Sparkling wine
is the specialty, but Washington's
only distillery is also located here.

# Winery Listings & Maps

WINE IS MUCH MORE THAN JUST A DRINK. WINE IS ABOUT people, places and culture. To help you meet those people, discover those places and share that culture, we've gathered together information on all the wineries in Washington and included it in this section, along with maps that will help you discover the magnificent terroir.

We've divided the state into separate areas to make the maps more useful and manageable. If you're looking for information on a particular winery but aren't sure which area it's in, consult the index.

Despite our best efforts to provide up-to-date information, it's important to remember that new wineries are constantly opening and existing wineries may adjust their hours of operation, close down or change their names. Every effort has been made to include complete and accurate information about every winery operating in Washington, but to avoid disappointment it pays to call in advance when you plan to visit a winery.

Wine touring is an enjoyable way to explore the country and taste the fruits of the land, but we always recommend having a designated driver. An excellent way to reward your driver is to buy them lunch at a winery or buy them a bottle or two of the wines you've tried that day.

The wine industry in Washington is worth more than $3 billion annually and supports in excess of 14,000 jobs. The wineries scattered throughout the state all have their own unique personality. The wines themselves provide some insight, but there's no better way to understand the industry than to visit the wineries yourself, talk to the people who make the wine and let their passion inspire you.

With more than 300 wineries currently in operation, there's a lot to see and taste. The diverse wine landscapes, ranging from deserts to mountains and rugged coastal areas to lush, fertile valleys, make the travels every bit as enjoyable as the tasting. Your adventure is just beginning, so get out there and enjoy the spectacular, winding wine roads of Washington.

# Driving Distances

*(Approximate times with good driving conditions)*

BENTON CITY – WALLA WALLA: 70 miles, 1 hr 40 min

CHELAN – YAKIMA: 140 miles, 3 hrs

GOLDENDALE – SEATTLE: 215 miles, 3 hrs 40 min

ISSAQUAH – SEATTLE: 18 miles, 25 min

LEAVENWORTH – SEATTLE: 120 miles, 2 hrs 25 min

OROVILLE – OSOYOOS (Canada): 8 miles, 15 min (excludes border crossing wait)

PORT ANGELES – YAKIMA: 230 miles, 5 hrs (includes ferry)

PORTLAND – SEATTLE: 175 miles, 3 hrs

PROSSER – SPOKANE: 170 miles, 3 hrs

SEATTLE – BENTON CITY: 210 miles, 3 hrs 30 min

SEATTLE – CHELAN: 180 miles, 3 hrs 40 min

SEATTLE – SPOKANE: 280 miles, 4 hrs 30 min

SEATTLE – WALLA WALLA: 280 miles, 5 hrs

SEATTLE – WOODINVILLE: 20 miles, 30 min

SEATTLE – PORT ANGELES: 85 miles, 2 hrs 30 min (includes ferry)

VANCOUVER (Canada) – SEATTLE: 140 miles, 2 hrs 30 min (excludes border crossing wait)

WALLA WALLA – GOLDENDALE: 160 miles, 3 hrs

WALLA WALLA – YAKIMA: 130 miles, 2 hrs 30 min

YAKIMA – PROSSER: 50 miles, 1 hr

YAKIMA – SEATTLE: 145 miles, 2 hrs 25 min

# Wineries of the Puget Sound and Seattle Area

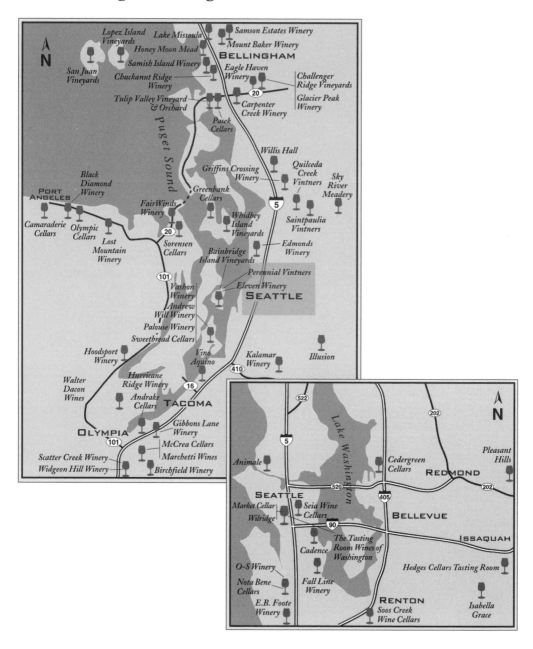

## Wineries of the Puget Sound and Seattle Area

ALDER RIDGE
600 University Street, Suite 2500
Seattle
(206) 728 9063
www.corusestates.com
Hours: Not open to the public

ANDRAKE CELLARS
6315 Boston Harbour Road NE
Olympia
(360) 943 3746
www.andrakecellars.com
Hours: Not open to the public

ANDREW WILL WINERY
12526 SW Bank Road, Vashon Island
(206) 463 9227
www.andrewwill.com
Hours: Not open to the public

ANIMALE
P.O Box 70491, Seattle
(206) 782 8047
www.animalewine.com
Hours: By appointment

ARBUTUS WINERY
West Seattle
(206) 498 3348
www.arbutuswinery.com
Hours: Not yet open to the public but
check for updated details

AVERY LANE
3534 Bagley Ave N, Seattle
(206) 267 5252
www.averylanewine.com
Hours: By appointment

BAINBRIDGE ISLAND VINEYARDS
& WINERY
8989 E Day Road, Bainbridge Island
(206) 842 9463
www.bainbridgevineyards.com
Hours: Fri.–Sun. 11 a.m.–5 p.m. or by
appointment

BIRCHFIELD WINERY
921 Middle Fork Road, Onalaska
(360) 978 5224
Hours: By appointment

BLACK DIAMOND WINERY
2976 Black Diamond Road
Port Angeles
(360) 457 0748
http://pages.prodigy.net/sharonlance
Hours: Open Thu.–Sat. 10 a.m.–5 p.m.,
Sun. and Mon. 11 a.m.–4 p.m.
Closed Jan.

BRIAN CARTER CELLARS
At time of going to press, this winery
was planning a move to Woodinville.
(425) 806 9463
www.briancartercellars.com
Hours: Call for details

CADENCE
2920 6th Avenue South, Seattle
(206) 381 9507
www.cadencewinery.com
Hours: By appointment

CAMARADERIE CELLARS
334 Benson Road, Port Angeles
(360) 417 3564
www.camaraderiecellars.com
Hours: May–Sep. Fri.–Sun.
11 a.m.–5 p.m.

CARPENTER CREEK WINERY
20376 E Hickox Road, Mount Vernon
(360) 848 6673
www.carpentercreek.com
Hours: Fri.–Sat. 10 a.m.–6 p.m.

CEDERGREEN CELLARS
11315 NE 65th Street, Kirkland
(425) 827 7244
www.cedargreencellars.com
Hours: Not open to the public

CHALLENGER RIDGE VINEYARD
& CELLARS
43095 Challenger Road, Concrete
(360) 853 7360
www.challegerridge.com
Hours: Weekends noon–5 p.m.

CHATTER CREEK WINERY
620 NE 55th Street, Seattle
(206) 985 2816
www.chattercreek.com
Hours: By appointment

CHUCKANUT RIDGE WINE CO.
3211 Chuckanut Drive, Bow
(360) 766 4336
www.chuckanutridge.net
Hours: By appointment

COUGAR CREEK WINE
Fall City
(425) 222 6546
www.cougarcreekwine.com
Hours: By appointment, call for
directions

CRUTCHER CELLARS
24707 SE 45th Place, Issaquah
(425) 417 0115
www.crutchercellars.com
Hours: By appointment

E.B. FOOTE WINERY
127-B SW 153rd Street, Burien
(206) 242 3852
www.ebfootewinery.com
Hours: Fri. and Sat. 10 a.m.–4 p.m.,
Tue. and Thu. 7 p.m.–9 p.m.
or by appointment

EAGLE HAVEN WINERY
8243 Sims Road, Sedro Woolley
(360) 856 6248
www.eaglehavenwinery.com
Hours: Fri.–Mon. 11 a.m.–5 p.m.
or by appointment

EDMONDS WINERY
1010 Spruce Street, Edmonds
(425) 774 8959
www.edmondswinery.com
Hours: By appointment

ELEVEN WINERY
12976 Roe Road NE, Bainbridge Island
(206) 780 0905
www.elevenwinery.com
Hours: By appointment

FAIR WINDS WINERY
1984 Hastings Ave., W.
Port Townsend
(360) 385 6899
www.fairwindswinery.com
Hours: Jun.–Sep. daily, Sep.–May,
Fri.–Mon., always noon–5 p.m.

FALL LINE WINERY
6122 6th Avenue, Seattle
(206) 768 9463
www.falllinewinery.com
Hours: By appointment

GIBBONS LANE WINERY/DONEDEI
PO BOX 7755, Olympia
(360) 264 8466
www.donedei.com
Hours: By appointment

GLACIER PEAK WINERY
58575 State Route 20, Rockport
(360) 770 9811
www.glacierpeakwinery.com
Hours: May–Sep. weekends
11 a.m.–5 p.m., also open holidays
and by appointment

GREENBANK CELLARS
Greenbank Farm, 3112 S Day Road
Greenbank
(360) 678 3964
www.whidbey.com/wine
Hours: Thu.–Mon. 11 a.m.–5 p.m.

GRIFFINS CROSSING WINERY
1802 131st DR NE, Lake Stevens
(425) 876 2396
www.griffinscrossing.com
Hours: Open by appointment

HEDGES CELLARS TASTING ROOM
195 NE Gilman Blvd, Issaquah
(425) 391 6056
www.hedgescellars.com
Hours: Mar.–Nov., Fri.–Sun.
11 a.m.–5 p.m.

HESTIA CELLARS
PO Box 1165, Carnation
(425) 333 4270
www.hestiacellars.com
Hours: Not open to the public

HONEY MOON MEAD, CIDER
& WINE
1053 N State Street, Bellingham
(360) 734 0728
www.honeymoonmead.net
Hours: Wed.–Fri. 5 p.m.–11 p.m., Sat.
3 p.m.–11 p.m., Sun. 3 p.m.–9 p.m.

HOODSPORT WINERY
N 23501 Highway 101, Hoodsport
(360) 877 9894
www.hoodsport.com
Hours: Daily 10 a.m.–6 p.m.

HURRICANE RIDGE WINERY
4309 Glen Terra Drive SE, Olympia
(360) 459 1638
Hours: By appointment

ILLUSION
32446 Morgan Drive, Black Diamond
(206) 261 1682
www.illusionwine.com
Hours: By appointment. See website
for details as a new tasting room is
planned sometime in 2007.

ISABELLA GRACE WINERY
28611 SE 204th Street, Hobart
(425) 941 6364
www.isabellagracewinery.com
Hours: By appointment

KALAMAR WINERY
5906 218th Avenue East, Sumner
(253) 862 9844
www.kalamarwinery.com
Hours: By appointment

LAHAR WINERY
16163 State Route 536, Mount Vernon
(360) 428 6894
www.laharwines.com
Hours: Call for hours and directions

LAKE MISSOULA WINE CO.
1625 Boblett Street, Blaine
(360) 332 2097
www.lakemissoulawine.com
Hours: By appointment

LOPEZ ISLAND VINEYARDS
724 Fisherman Bay Road, Lopez Island
(360) 468 3644
www.lopezislandvineyards.com
Hours: Jul.–Aug., Wed.–Sat., May, Jun.
and Sep., Fri.–Sat. and Apr., Oct.–Dec.
16, Sat. only. Hours always
noon–5 p.m.

LOST MOUNTAIN WINERY
3174 Lost Mountain Road, Sequim
(360) 683 5229
www.lostmountain.com
Hours: From mid-Jun.–mid-Sep.,
daily 11 a.m.–5 p.m. Call for out of
season hours

MARCHETTI WINES
3709 Fuller Lane SE, Olympia
(360) 438 8851
www.marchettiwines.com
Hours: Not open to the public

MARKET CELLAR WINERY
1432 Western Avenue, Seattle
(206) 622 1880
www.marketcellarwinery.com
Hours: Mon.–Sat. 11 a.m.–6 p.m.

MCCREA CELLARS
7533 34th Avenue SW, Seattle
(206) 938 8643
www.mccreacellars.com
Hours: By appointment

MOUNT BAKER VINEYARDS
& WINERY
4298 Mount Baker Highway, Everson
(360) 592 2300
Hours: Daily 11 a.m.–5 p.m.

NOTA BENE CELLARS
4251 NE 88th Street, Seattle
(206) 459 2785
www.notabenecellars.com
Hours: By appointment

OLYMPIC CELLARS
255410 Highway 101, Port Angeles
(360) 452 0160
www.olympiccellars.com
Hours: May–Oct., daily 11 a.m.–
6 p.m.; Nov.–Apr., Mon.–Fri. and
Sun. 11 a.m.–5 p.m.

OS WINERY
1801 South 92nd Place, Suite B, Seattle
(206) 243 3427
www.oswinery.com
Hours: By appointment

PALOUSE WINERY
12431 Vashon Highway SW, Vashon
(206) 567 4994
www.palousewinery.com
Hours: By appointment

PASEK CELLARS
18729 Fir Island Road, Conway
(360) 445 4048
www.pasekcellars.com
Hours: Daily 11 a.m.–5 p.m.

PERENNIAL VINTNERS
8840 Lovgren Road, Bainbridge Island
(206) 780 2146
www.perennialvintners.com
Hours: By appointment

PLEASANT HILL WINERY
32305 NE 8th Street, Carnation
(425) 333 6770
www.pleasanthillestate.com
Hours: By appointment

PRECEPT BRANDS
3534 Bagley Avenue Nth, Seattle
(206) 267 5252
www.preceptbrands.com
Hours: Not open to the public

QUILCEDA CREEK VINTNERS
11306 52nd Street SE, Snohomish
(360) 568 2389
www.quilcedacreek.com
Hours: Not open to the public

RANDALL HARRIS WINES
3051 42nd Ave West, Seattle
(206) 283 7688
Hours: Not open to the public

SAINTPAULIA VINTNERS
18302 83rd Avenue SE, Snohomish
(360) 668 8585
www.saintpauliavintners.com
Hours: By appointment

SAMISH ISLAND WINERY
10990 Samish Island Road, Bow
(360) 766 6086
Hours: Not open to the public

SAMSON ESTATE WINERY
1861 Van Dyk Road, Everson
(360) 966 7787
www.samsonestates.com
Hours: Jun. 1-Sep. 30, daily 11 a.m.-
6 p.m.; Oct. 1-May 30 weekends
11 a.m.-5 p.m. or by appointment

SAN JUAN VINEYARDS
3136 Roche Harbor Road
Friday Harbor
(360) 378 9463
www.sanjuanvineyards.com
Hours: Daily 11 a.m.-5 p.m.
(seasonal so call ahead)

SCATTER CREEK WINERY
3442 180th Ave SW, Tenino
(360) 870 4092
Hours: By appointment

SEIA WINE CELLARS
431 25th Ave East, Seattle
(206) 250 9095
www.seiawines.com
Hours: Not open to the public

SKY RIVER MEADERY
32533 Cascade View Drive, Sultan
(360) 793 6761
www.skyriverbrewing.com
Hours: Mon.-Fri. 10 a.m.-4 p.m.

SOOS CREEK WINE CELLARS
20404 140th Avenue SE, Kent
(253) 631 8775
www.sooscreekwine.com
Hours: Annual open house only,
check website for details

SORENSON CELLARS
274 Otto Street, Port Townsend
(360) 379 6416
www.sorensencellars.com
Hours: Mar.-Nov., Fri.-Sun.
noon-5 p.m.

SWEETBREAD CELLARS
10730 SW 116th Street, Vashon Island
(509) 567 5769
www.sweetbreadcellars.com
Hours: Thu.-Sun. 10 a.m.-6 p.m.

TULIP VALLEY VINEYARD
& ORCHARD
16163 State Route 536, Mount Vernon
(360) 428 6894
www.redbarncider.com
Hours: Fri.-Sun. noon-6 p.m.

VASHON WINERY
10317 SW 156th Street, Vashon
(206) 567 0055
www.vashonwinery.com
Hours: May Day-Labor Day, Sat.
2 p.m.-5 p.m.

VINO AQUINO
2607 6th Ave, Tacoma
(253) 272 5511
www.vinoaquino.com
Hours: Mon.-Sat. 10 a.m.-6 p.m.

WALTER DACON
50 SE Skookum Inlet Road, Shelton
(360) 426 5913
www.walterdaconwines.com
Hours: Wed.-Sun. noon-6 p.m.

WARD JOHNSON WINERY
1405 Elliot Avenue West, Suite F2
Seattle
(206) 229 3421
www.wardjohnsonwinery.com
Hours: By appointment

WASHINGTON HILLS CELLARS
3534 Bagley Avenue Nth, Seattle
(206) 267 5252
www.washingtonhills.com
Hours: By appointment (not open
to the public at time of press)

WHIDBEY ISLAND VINEYARD
& WINERY
5237 S Langley Road, Langley
(360) 221 2040
www.whidbeyislandwinery.com
Hours: Wed.-Mon. noon-5 p.m.
(closed Mon. during winter)

WIDGEON HILL WINERY
121 Widgeon Hill Road, Chehalis
(360) 748 0432
www.widgeonhill.com
Hours: Call for current hours

WILLIS HALL
4715 126th Street NE, Marysville
(360) 653 1247
www.wilishall.com
Hours: By appointment

WILRIDGE WINERY
1416 34th Avenue, Seattle
(206) 325 3051
www.wilridgewinery.com
Hours: Not open to the public

WINES OF WASHINGTON
TASTING ROOM
1924 Post Alley. Pike Market Place
Seattle
(206) 770 9463
www.winesofwashington.com
Hours: Daily noon-8 p.m.

ZEFINA WINERY
600 University Street, Suite 2500
Seattle
(206) 728 9063 ext. 209
www.zefina.com
Hours: Not open to the public

# Wineries of the Woodinville Area

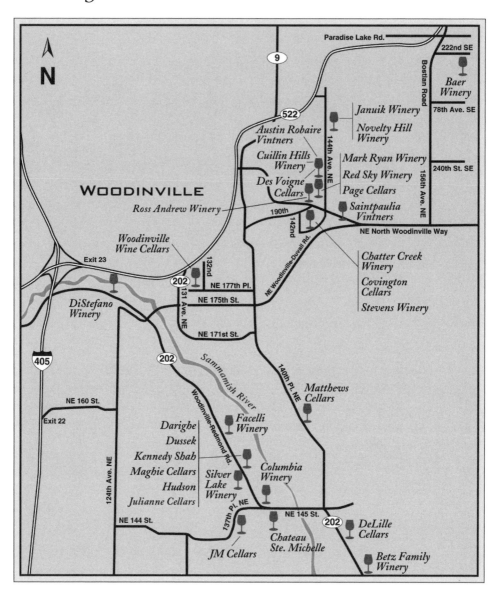

## Wineries of the Woodinville Area

ADYTUM CELLARS
15132 148th Ave NE, Woodinville
(425) 482 9030
www.adytum.com
Hours: Not open to the public

ARLINGTON ROAD CELLARS
19495 144th Ave NE Suite A-115
Woodinville
(425) 482 1801
www.arlingtonroadcellars.com
Hours: Not open to the public

AUSTIN ROBAIRE VINTNERS
19501 144th Avenue NE, Suite D-800
Woodinville
(206) 406 0360
www.austinrobaire.com
Hours: 1st and 3rd Sat. of every
month 1 p.m.–4 p.m.

BAER WINERY
9118 222nd Street SE, Woodinville
(425) 483 7060
www.baerwinery.com
Hours: Not open to the public

BETZ FAMILY WINERY
13244 Woodinville-Redmond Road
NE, Redmond
(425) 861 9823
www.betzfamilywinery.com
Hours: Open for visitors twice a year
on release weekends, check website
for details

CHATEAU STE. MICHELLE
14111 NE 145th Street, Woodinville
(425) 415 3300
www.ste-michelle.com
Hours: Open daily 10 a.m.–4:30 p.m.

COLUMBIA WINERY
14030 NE 145th Street, Woodinville
(425) 488 2776
www.columbiawinery.com
Hours: Daily, Oct.-Feb., 10 a.m.-5
p.m., summer 10 a.m.-7 p.m.

COVEY RUN VINTNERS
Woodinville
1 (888) 659 7900
www.coveyrun.com
Hours: Not open to the public

CUILLIN HILLS WINERY
19501 144th Avenue NE Suite C-200
Woodinville
(425) 415 8466
www.cuillinhills.com
Hours: Sat. noon-4 p.m.

DARIGHE
15500 Woodinville-Redmond Road
Suite C-600, Woodinville
(425) 527 0608
www.darighe.com
Hours: By appointment

DELILLE CELLARS/CHALEUR ESTATE
14208 Woodinville-Redmond Road
Woodinville
(425) 489 0544
www.delillecellars.com
Hours: By appointment

DES VOIGNE CELLARS
19501 144th Avenue NE, Suite C-200
Woodinville
(425) 415 8466
www.desvoignecellars.com
Hours: Call for details

DI STEFANO WINERY
12280 Woodinville Drive NE
Woodinville
(425) 487 1648
www.distefanowinery.com
Hours: Weekends noon-5 p.m.
or by appointment

DOMAINE STE. MICHELLE
14111 NE 145th, Woodinville
1 (866) 701 3187
www.domainestemichelle.com
Hours: Daily 10 a.m.–4:30 p.m.

DOYENNE AT DELILLE CELLARS
Woodinville
(425) 489 0544
www.doyennecellars.com
Hours: By appointment only,
call for details

DUSSECK FAMILY CELLARS
15500 Woodinville-Redmond Road
Suite C-600, Woodinville
(425) 527 0608
www.woodhousefamilycellars.com
Hours: By appointment

EROICA
14111 NE 145th, Woodinville
(425) 488 1133
www.ste-michelle.com
Hours: Daily 10 a.m.-4:30 p.m.

FACELLI WINERY
16120 Woodinville/Redmond Road NE
#1, Woodinville
(425) 488 1020
www.facelliwinery.com
Hours: Weekends noon-4 p.m.

JANUIK WINERY
19730 144th Ave NE, Woodinville
(425) 481 5502
www.januikwinery.com
Hours: Check website or call
for details

JM CELLARS
14404 137th Place NE, Woodinville
(206) 321 0052
www.jmcellars.com
Hours: First Sat. of every month
noon-4 p.m.

JU'LIANNE CELLARS
15500 Woodinville-Redmond Road,
Suite C-600, Woodinville
(425) 283 7140
Hours: By appointment

KENNEDY SHAH CELLARS
15500 Woodinville-Redmond Road
Suite C-600, Woodinville
(425) 527 0608
www.kennedyshah.com
Hours: Fri. noon-4 p.m., weekends
noon-5 p.m. or by appointment

MAGHIE CELLARS
15500 Woodinville-Redmond Road
Suite C-600, Woodinville
(425) 527 0608
www.woodhousefamilycellars.com
Hours: By appointment

MARK RYAN WINERY
19501 144th Ave NE #F900
Woodinville
(206) 910 7967
www.markryanwinery.com
Hours: By appointment

MATTHEWS CELLARS
16116 140th Place NE, Woodinville
(425) 487 9810
www.matthewscellars.com
Hours: Sat. noon–4 p.m.

NOVELTY HILL WINERY
14710 Woodinville-Redmond Highway
Woodinville
(425) 481 5502
www.noveltyhillwines.com
Hours: Open daily. Call or check
website for hours

PAGE CELLARS
19495 144th Avenue NE Suite B235
Woodinville
(253) 232 9463
www.pagecellars.com
Hours: Sat. noon–4 p.m.

PAUL THOMAS WINERY
PO Box 1248, Woodinville
(425) 488 8164
www.paulthomaswinery.com
Hours: Not open to the public

RED SKY WINERY
19495 144th Ave NE, Woodinville
(425) 481 9864
www.redskywinery.com
Hours: By appointment

ROSS ANDREW WINERY
18512 142nd Avenue NE, Woodinville
(206) 369 3615
www.rossandrewwinery.com
Hours: By appointment, call for details

SAINTPAULIA VINTNERS
TASTING ROOM
14522 NE Woodinville Way
Woodinville
(360) 668 8585
www.saintpauliavintners.com
Hours: Sat. noon–5 p.m.

SILVER LAKE WINERY
15029 Woodinville-Redmond Road
Woodinville
(425) 485 2437
www.silverlakewinery.com
Hours: Daily 11 a.m.–5 p.m.

STEVENS WINERY
18510 142nd Ave NE, Woodinville
(425) 424 9463
www.stevenswinery.com
Hours: Sat. noon–4:30 p.m.

VINE & SUN
PO Box 167, Woodinville
(425) 398 7147
www.vineandsun.com
Hours: Not open to the public

WOODHOUSE FAMILY CELLARS
15500 Woodinville-Redmond Road
Suite C-600, Woodinville
(425) 527 0608
www.woodhousefamilycellars.com
Hours: Fri. noon–4 p.m., weekends
noon–5 p.m. or by appointment

## Wineries of the Yakima Valley Area

AGATE FIELD VINEYARD
2911 Roza Drive, Zillah
(509) 930 0806
www.agatefieldvineyard.com
Hours: Apr.–mid-Dec., Fri.–Sun.
11 a.m.–5 p.m.

ALEXANDRIA NICOLE WINERY
2880 Lee Road, Suite C, Prosser
(509) 786 3497
www.alexandrianicolecellars.com
Hours: Daily 11 a.m.–5 p.m.

APEX CELLARS
111 East Lincoln Avenue, Sunnyside
(509) 839 9463
www.apexcellars.com
Hours: Summer hours daily 10 a.m.–
5 p.m., Winter hours Thu.–Mon.
11 a.m. –5 p.m.

BONAIR WINERY
500 S Bonair Road, Zillah
(509) 829 6027
www.bonairwine.com
Hours: Open daily 10 a.m.–5 p.m.

BRIDGMAN CELLARS
111 East Lincoln Avenue, Sunnyside
(509) 839 9463
www.apexcellars.com
Hours: Summer hours daily 10 a.m.–
5 p.m., Winter hours Thu.–Mon.
11 a.m. –5 p.m.

BUNNELL FAMILY CELLAR
87203 West 134 PR NW, Prosser
(509) 973 4187
www.riveraerie.com
Hours: By appointment

C.R. SANDIDGE WINES
2880 Lee Road, Prosser
(509) 786 1100
www.crsandidgewines.com
Hours: Wed.–Sun. 10 a.m.–5 p.m.
or by appointment

CANYON'S EDGE WINERY
1095 Hale Road, Mabton
(509) 772 2179
www.canyonsedgewinery.com
Hours: Call for details

CHATEAU CHAMPOUX
524 Alderdale Road, Prosser
(509) 894 5005
www.chateauchampoux.com
Hours: Jun.–Nov. by appointment

CHINOOK WINES
Wine Country Road at Wittkopf Loop
Prosser
(509) 786 2725
www.chinookwines.com
Hours: May–Oct. weekends
noon–5 p.m.

CLAAR CELLARS TASTING ROOM
1001 Vintage Valley Parkway, Zillah
(509) 829 6810
www.claarcellars.com
Hours: Mar.–Oct. 10 a.m.–6 p.m.,
Nov.–Feb. 11 a.m.–5 p.m.

CÔTE BONNEVILLE
2841 Fordyce Road, Sunnyside
(509) 840 4596
www.cotebonneville.com
Hours: By appointment

COVENTRY VALE WINERY
Wilgus and Evans Roads, Grandview
(509) 882 4100
Hours: By appointment

COVINGTON CELLARS
18580 142nd Avenue, Woodinville
(425) 806 8636
www.covingtoncellars.com
Hours: Sat. 1 p.m.–5 p.m. or
by appointment

COWAN VINEYARDS
2880 Lee Road Suite E, Prosser
(509) 788 0200
www.cowanvineyards.com
Hours: Summer Thu.–Mon. 10 a.m.–
5 p.m., winter on weekends
noon–4 p.m.

COYOTE CANYON WINERY
717 Sixth Street, Prosser
(509) 786 7686
www.coyotecanyonwinery.com
Hours: Tue.–Thu. 11 a.m.–6 p.m., Fri.
and Sat. 11 a.m.–7 p.m.

# Wineries of the Yakima Valley Area

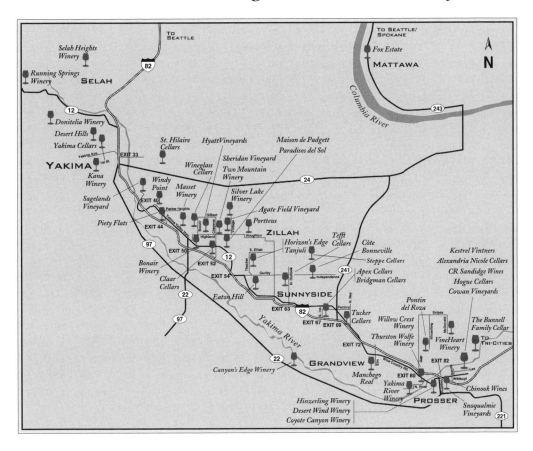

**DESERT HILLS**
Solutec Complex, 1208 North 1st
Street, Yakima
(509) 453 0503
www.deserthillswinery.com
Hours: Mon.-Fri. 10 a.m.-5 p.m.,
weekends noon-4 p.m.
or by appointment

**DESERT WIND VINEYARD & WINERY**
2258 Wine Country Road, Prosser
1 (800) 437 3213
www.desertwindvineyard.com
Hours: Visitors welcome,
call for details

**DONITELIA WINERY**
10 N 6th Avenue, Yakima
(509) 452 9900
www.donitelia.com
Hours: Fri. 4 p.m.-7 p.m., Sat. noon-
5 p.m. and by appointment

**EATON HILL WINERY**
530 Gurley Road, Granger
(509) 854 2220
Hours: Daily 10 a.m.-5 p.m.

**FOX ESTATE WINERY**
24962 Highway 243 South, Mattawa
(509) 932 5818
www.foxestatewinery.com
Hours: Mon.-Fri. 10 a.m.-5 p.m.
During summer also open weekends
noon-4 p.m.

**HINZERLING WINERY**
1520 Sheridan, Prosser
(509) 786 2163
www.hinzerling.com
Hours: Mon.-Sat. 11 a.m.-5 p.m., Sun.
11 a.m.-4 p.m. Closed Jan.-Feb. and on
Sun. during winter.

**HOGUE CELLARS**
2800 Lee Road, Prosser
1 (800) 565 9779
www.hoguecellars.com
Hours: Summer open daily 10 a.m.-
5 p.m., call for winter hours

**HORIZON'S EDGE WINERY**
4530 East Zillah Drive, Zillah
(509) 829 6401
www.horizonsedgewinery.com
Hours: Fri.-Mon. 11 a.m.-5 p.m.
Closed Dec.-Feb.

**HYATT VINEYARDS WINERY**
2020 Gilbert Road, Zillah
(509) 829 6333
www.hyattvineyards.com
Hours: Daily 11 a.m.-5 p.m.

KANA WINERY
10 South 2nd Street, Yakima
(509) 453 6611
www.kanawinery.com
Hours: Mon.-Sat. noon-6:30 p.m.,
Sun. noon-5 p.m. Closed Mon.
during winter.

KESTREL VINTNERS
Prosser Wine & Food Park
2890 Lee Road, Prosser
(509) 786 2675
www.kestrelwines.com
Hours: Daily 10 a.m.-5 p.m.

MAISON DE PADGETT WINERY
2231 Rosa Drive, Zillah
(509) 829 6412
www.maisondepadgettwinery.com
Hours: Thu.-Mon. 11 a.m.-5 p.m.
Closed Dec.-Mar.

MANCHEGO REAL
604 Elm Street, Grandview
(509) 882 6111
www.manchegoreal.com
Hours: Daily 10 a.m.-4 p.m. or by
appointment

MCKINLEY SPRINGS
1201 Alderdale Road, Prosser
(509) 894 4528
www.mckinleysprings.com
Hours: Sat. 10 a.m.-6 p.m.
or by appointment

MASSET WINERY
620 E Parker Heights Road, Wapato
(509) 877 6675
www.massetwinery.com
Hours: Feb.-Nov. free tastings Thu.-
Sun. 11 a.m.-5 p.m. Call to confirm.

PARADISOS DEL SOL WINERY
3230 Highland Drive, Zillah
(509) 829 9000
www.paradisosdelsol.com
Hours: Daily 11 a.m.-6 p.m.

PIETY FLATS WINERY
The Donald Fruit & Mercantile, 2560
Donald Wapato Road, Wapato
(509) 877 3115
www.pietyflatswinery.com
Hours: Mar.-Dec. daily 10 a.m.-6 p.m.
(5 p.m. on Sun. and daily Nov.-Dec.),
weekends only Jan.-Feb.

PORTTEUS VINEYARDS & WINERY
5201 Highland Drive, Zillah
(509) 829 6970
www.portteus.com
Hours: Daily 10 a.m.-5 p.m. (opens at
11 a.m. on weekends)

RUNNING SPRING'S WINE
Thompson's Farm Market 9950
Highway 12, Naches
(509) 653 2848
Hours: Jun.-Oct., daily 10 a.m.-5 p.m.,
Apr.-May, weekends 10 a.m.-5 p.m.

SAGELANDS VINEYARD & WINERY
71 Gangl Road, Wapato
1 (800) 967 8115
www.sagelandsvineyard.com
Hours: Daily 10 a.m.-5 p.m. (during
winter closes at 4 p.m.)

SELAH HEIGHTS WINERY
31 Katie Lane, Selah
(509) 698 6980
www.selahheightswinery.com
Hours: Memorial Day-Christmas,
weekends or by appointment,
call for hours

SHERIDAN VINEYARD
2980 Gilbert Road, Zillah
(509) 829 3205
www.sheridanvineyard.com
Hours: Apr.-Nov., Fri. and Sat.
11 a.m.-5 p.m., Sun. noon-4 p.m.

SILVER LAKE WINERY AT
ROZA HILLS
1500 Vintage Road, Zillah
(509) 829 6235
www.silverlakewinery.com
Hours: Apr.-Nov. daily 10 a.m.-5 p.m.,
Dec.-Mar., 11 a.m.-4 p.m.

SNOQUALMIE VINEYARDS
660 Frontier Road, Prosser
1 (800) 852 0885
www.snoqualmie.com
Hours: Daily 10 a.m.-5 p.m.

STEPPE CELLARS
1991 Chaffee Road, Sunnyside
(509) 837 8281
www.steppecellars.com
Hours: Call for hours

ST. HILAIRE CELLARS
1340 St Hilaire Road, Yakima
(509) 453 5987
Hours: By appointment

TANJULI
4530 East Zillah Drive, Zillah
(406) 883 0803
Hours: By appointment

TEFFT CELLARS WINERY AND
GUEST HOUSE
1320 Independence Road, Outlook
(509) 837 7651
www.tefftcellars.com
Hours: Daily 10 a.m.-5 p.m.

THURSTON WOLFE WINERY
588 Cabernet Court, Prosser
(509) 786 1764
www.thurstonwolfe.com
Hours: Mar. 1-Dec. 10, Thu.-Sun.
11 a.m.-5 p.m. (also open
holiday Mon.)

TUCKER CELLARS
70 Ray Road, Sunnyside
(509) 837 8701
www.tuckercellars.com
Hours: Daily 10 a.m.-5 p.m.

TWO MOUNTAIN WINERY
2151 Cheyne Road, Zillah
(509) 829 3900
www.twomountainwinery.com
Hours: Open daily between President's
Day-Dec. 1, 10 a.m.-6 p.m.

VINEHEART WINERY
44209 N McDonald Road, Prosser
(509) 973 2993
www.vineheart.com
Hours: Thu.-Mon. 9 a.m.-5 p.m.

WILLOW CREST WINERY
590 Merlot Drive, Prosser
(509) 786 7999
www.willowcrestwinery.com
Hours: Daily 10 a.m.-5 p.m.

WINDY POINT VINEYARDS
420 Windy Point Drive, Wapato
(509) 877 6824
www.windypointvineyards.com
Hours: Thu.-Mon. 10 a.m.-5 p.m.
(Dec.-Jan. hours vary so call ahead)

WINEGLASS CELLARS
260 North Bonair Road, Zillah
(509) 829 3011
www.wineglasscellars.com
Hours: Thu.-Sun. 10:30 a.m.-5 p.m.
Closed Dec. 1-Feb. 14.

YAKIMA CELLARS
32 N 2nd Street, Yakima
(509) 577 0461
www.yakimacellars.com
Hours: Tue.-Sun. noon-6 p.m. or by
appointment

YAKIMA RIVER WINERY
143302 W North River Road, Prosser
(509) 786 2805
www.yakimariverwinery.com
Hours: Daily 10 a.m.-5 p.m.

# Wineries of the Tri-Cities Area

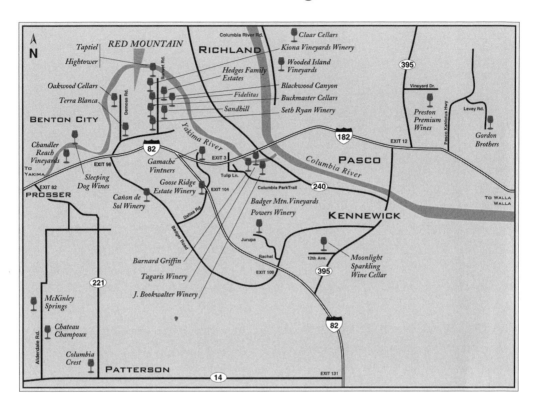

## WINERIES OF THE TRI-CITIES AREA

BADGER MOUNTAIN WINERY
1106 South Jurupa Street, Kennewick
1 (800) 643 9463
www.badgermtnvineyard.com
Hours: Daily 10 a.m.–5 p.m.

BARNARD GRIFFIN WINERY
878 Tulip Lane, Richland
(509) 627 0266
www.barnardgriffin.com
Hours: 10 a.m.–6 p.m. year-round

BLACKWOOD CANYON
53258 North Sunset Road, Benton City
(509) 588 7124
www.blackwoodwine.com
Hours: Daily 10 a.m.–6 p.m.

BUCKMASTER CELLARS
35802 N Sunset Road, Benton City
(509) 628 8474
www.buckmastercellars.com
Hours: Open for event weekends,
check website for details

CANON DE SOL WINERY
46415 E Badger Road, Benton City
(509) 588 6311
www.canondesol.com
Hours: By appointment

CHANDLER REACH VINEYARDS
& WINERY
9506 West Chandler Road
Benton City
(509) 588 8800
www.chandlerreach.com
Hours: Wed.–Sun. noon–5 p.m.

CLAAR CELLARS WINERY
1081 Glenwood Road
Matthews Corner, Pasco
(509) 266 4449
www.claarcellars.com
Hours: By appointment

COL SOLARE
At time of print winery is under
construction and address is non-
existent. Winery is on Red Mountain,
close to Hedges Family Estates.
(425) 488 1133
www.colsolare.com
Hours: Check website for details

COLUMBIA CREST WINERY
Highway 221, Columbia Crest Drive
Paterson
(509) 875 2061
www.columbiacrest.com
Hours: Daily 10 a.m.–4:30 p.m.

FIDELITAS
Sunset Road, Benton City
(509) 521 4433
www.fidelitaswines.com
Hours: Check website for details

GOOSE RIDGE ESTATE VINEYARDS
& WINERY
16304 North Dallas Road, Richland
(509) 628 3880
www.gooseridge.com
Hours: Thu.–Sun. 10 a.m.–6 p.m.

GORDON BROTHERS CELLARS
671 Levey Road, Pasco
(509) 547 6331
www.gordonwines.com
Hours: Not open to the public except
by appointment and on special
occasions

HEDGES FAMILY ESTATE
53511 North Sunset Road, Benton City
(509) 588 3155
www.hedgesfamilyestate.com
Hours: Mar.–Nov., Fri.–Sun.
11 a.m.–5 p.m.

HIGHTOWER CELLARS
19418 East 583 PR NE, Benton City
(509) 588 2867
www.hightowercellars.com
Hours: By appointment and on
event weekends

J. BOOKWALTER WINERY
894 Tulip Lane, Richland
(509) 627 5000
www.bookwalterwines.com
Hours: Mon.–Tue. 10 a.m.–8 p.m.,
Wed.–Sat. 10 a.m.–11 p.m., Sun.
10 a.m.–6 p.m.

KIONA VINEYARDS AND WINERY
44612 North Sunset Road, Benton City
(509) 588 6716
www.kionawine.com
Hours: Daily noon–5 p.m. except
major holidays

MOONLIGHT SPARKLING
WINE CELLAR
4704 W 12th Avenue, Kennewick
(509) 735 7237
www.moonlightcellar.com
Hours: By appointment

OAKWOOD CELLARS WINERY
40504 North Demoss Road
Benton City
(509) 588 5332
www.oakwoodcellars.com
Hours: Presidents Day Weekend–mid-
Dec., Fri.–Sun. noon–5 p.m. Otherwise
by appointment

PONTIN DEL ROZA
35502 North Hinzerling Road, Prosser
(509) 786 4449
Hours: Daily 10 a.m.–5 p.m.

POWERS WINERY
1106 South Jurupa Street, Kennewick
1 (800) 643 9463
www.powerswinery.com
Hours: Daily 10 a.m.–5 p.m.

PRESTON PREMIUM WINES
502 East Vineyard Drive, Pasco
(509) 545 1990 ext. 10
www.prestonwines.com
Hours: Daily 10 a.m.–5:30 p.m.

SANDHILL WINERY
48313 North Sunset Road, Benton City
(360) 887 5629
Hours: Weekends 11 a.m.–5 p.m.
except Christmas and New Year's Day

SETH RYAN WINERY
35306 Sunset Road, Benton City
(509) 588 6780
www.sethryan.com
Hours: Apr.–Oct., daily 10 a.m.–6 p.m.;
Nov.–Mar., daily noon–5 p.m.

SLEEPING DOG WINES
45804 N Whitmore PR NW
Benton City
(509) 460 2886
www.sleepingdogwines.com
Hours: By appointment

TAGARIS WINERY
844 Tulip Lane, Richland
(509) 628 0020
www.tagariswines.com
Hours: Open but call ahead for details

TAPTEIL VINEYARD WINERY
20206 E 583 PR N.E, Benton City
(509) 588 4460
www.tapteil.com
Hours: Apr.–Dec., Sat. 11 a.m.–5 p.m.

TERRA BLANCA WINERY AND
ESTATE VINEYARD
34715 N Demoss Road, Benton City
(509) 588 6082
www.terrablanca.com
Hours: Daily 11 a.m.–6 p.m.

WOODED ISLAND VINEYARDS
91 N Columbia River Road, Pasco
(509) 542 0194
www.woodedislandvineyards.com
Hours: By appointment

## Wineries of the Walla Walla Area

ABEJA
2014 Mill Creek Road, Walla Walla
(509) 526 7400
www.abeja.net
Hours: By appointment

AMAURICE WINERY
178 Vineyard Lane, Walla Walla
(509) 522 5444
www.amaurice.com
Hours: By appointment

AMAVI CELLARS
635 N 13th Avenue, Walla Walla
(509) 525 3541
www.amavicellars.com
Hours: Daily 11 a.m.–5 p.m.

ASH HOLLOW WINERY
14 North 2nd Avenue, Walla Walla
(509) 529 7565
www.ashhollow.com
Hours: Wed.–Sat. noon–8 p.m., Sun.
noon–4 p.m. Winter hours may be
reduced, call for details.

BALBOA WINERY
4169 Pepper Bridge Road, Walla Walla
(509) 529 0461
www.balboawinery.com
Hours: Call for details

BASEL CELLARS ESTATE WINERY
2901 Old Milton Highway
Walla Walla
(509) 522 0200
www.baselcellars.com
Hours: Mon.–Sat. 10 a.m. –4 p.m., Sun.
11 a.m.–4 p.m. (Closed Sun. during
off season.)

BERESAN
4169 Pepper Bridge Road, Walla Walla
(509) 522 2395
www.beresanwines.com
Hours: Sat. 11 a.m.–4 p.m.
or by appointment

BERGEVIN LANE VINEYARDS
1215 West Poplar Street, Walla Walla
(509) 526 4300
www.bergevinlane.com
Hours: Mon.–Sat. 11 a.m.–4 p.m.

BUNCHGRASS WINERY
Bunchgrass Lane (Off Highway 12,
4 miles west of Walla Walla)
Walla Walla
(509) 525 1492
www.bunchgrasswinery.com
Hours: By appointment

# Wineries of the Walla Walla Area

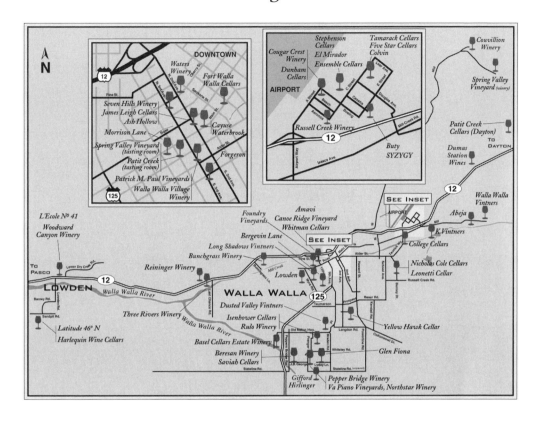

**BUTY WINERY**
535 E Cessna Ave, Walla Walla
(509) 527 0901
www.butywinery.com
Hours: Almost daily 11 a.m.–4 p.m.

**CANOE RIDGE VINEYARD**
1102 West Cherry Street, Walla Walla
(509) 527 0885
www.canoeridgevineyard.com
Hours: May–Sep., 11 a.m.–5 p.m.,
Oct.–Apr., 11 a.m.–4 p.m. Closed major
holidays and Dec. 24–Jan. 1.

**CAYUSE VINEYARDS**
17 E Main Street, Walla Walla
(509) 526 0686
www.cayusevineyards.com
Hours: By appointment

**COLLEGE CELLARS OF
WALLA WALLA**
500 Tausick Way, Walla Walla
(509) 524 5170
www.collegecellarsofwallawalla.com
Hours: By appointment only

**COLVIN VINEYARDS**
720 C Street Walla Walla Regional
Airport, Walla Walla
(509) 525 7802
www.colvinvineyards.com
Hours: Sat. 11 a.m.–4 p.m.
or by appointment

**COUGAR CREST WINERY**
202 A Street, Walla Walla
(509) 529 5980
www.cougarcrestwinery.com
Hours: Summer Thu.–Sat. 11 a.m.–
4 p.m., Fri.–Sun. 10 a.m.–3 p.m.
Winter by appointment.

**COUVILLION WINERY**
86 Corkrum Road, Walla Walla
(509) 337 6133
www.couvillionwinery.com
Hours: By appointment

**DUMAS STATION WINES**
36229 Highway 12, Dayton
(509) 382 8933
www.dumasstation.com
Hours: Call for details

**DUNHAM CELLARS**
150 E Boeing Ave, Walla Walla
Regional Airport
(509) 529 4685
www.dunhamcellars.com
Hours: Daily 11 a.m.–4 p.m.

**DUSTED VALLEY VINTNERS**
1248 Old Milton Highway
Walla Walla
(509)301 4470
www.dustedvalley.com
Hours: Weekends noon–5 p.m.

**EL MIRADOR**
425 "B" Street, Walla Walla
Regional Airport
(509) 526 0233
www.elmiradorwinery.com
Hours: Tue.–Sun. 10 a.m.–4 p.m.

ENSEMBLE CELLARS
145 East Curtis Avenue, Walla Walla
(509) 525 0231
www.ensemblecellars.com
Hours: By appointment

FIVE STAR CELLARS
840 "C" Street, Walla Walla
(509) 527 8400
www.fivestarcellars.com
Hours: Sat. 10 a.m.–4 p.m.
or by appointment

FORGERON CELLARS
33 West Birch Street, Walla Walla
(509) 522 9463
www.forgeroncellars.com
Hours: Daily 11 a.m.–4 p.m.
(Closed major holidays.)

FORT WALLA WALLA CELLARS
TASTING ROOM
127 E Main Street, Walla Walla
(509) 520 1095
www.fortwallawallacellars.com
Hours: Thu.–Mon. 10 a.m.–4:30 p.m.

FOUNDRY VINEYARDS
405 N.Woodland Ave, Walla Walla
(509) 529 0736
www.wallawallafoundry.com
Hours: Tue.–Sat. 10 a.m.–5 p.m.,
Sun. noon–4 p.m.

GIFFORD HIRLINGER
1459 Stateline Road, Walla Walla
(509) 301 9229
www.giffordhirlinger.com
Hours: Call for details

GLEN FIONA
1249 Lyday Lane, Walla Walla
(509) 522 2566
www.glenfiona.com
Hours: Weekends 11 a.m.–4 p.m.
and by appointment

HARLEQUIN CELLARS
1211 Sand Pit Road, Touchet
(509) 394 2112
www.harlequinwine.com
Hours: By appointment

ISENHOWER CELLARS
3471 Pranger Road, Walla Walla
(509) 526 7896
www.isenhowercellars.com
Hours: Weekends 10:30 a.m.–5 p.m.
or by appointment

JLC WINERY
16 N 2nd Avenue, Walla Walla
(509) 529 1398
www.jamesleighcellars.com
Hours: Weekends and by appointment

K VINTNERS
820 Mill Creek Road, Walla Walla
(509) 526 5230
www.kvintners.com
Hours: Apr.–Oct., Sat. 10 a.m.–5 p.m.

LATITUDE 46° N
1211 Sand Pit Road, Touchet
(509) 394 0460
www.latitude46.com
Hours: By appointment

L'ECOLE NO 41
41 Lowden School Road, PO Box 111
Lowden
(509) 525 0940
www.lecole.com
Hours: Daily 10 a.m.–5 p.m.

LEONETTI CELLAR
1875 Foothills Lane, Walla Walla
(509) 525 1428
www.leonetticellar.com
Hours: Not open to the public

LONG SHADOWS VINTNERS
(INCLUDES FEATHER, PIROUETTE,
SAGGI, PEDESTAL, POET'S LEAP,
CHESTER-KIDDER AND SEQUEL)
1215 West Poplar Street, Walla Walla
(509) 526 0905
www.longshadows.com
Hours: By appointment (2 weeks'
notice required)

LOWDEN HILLS WINERY
535 NE Spitzenburg Road
College Place
(509) 527 1040
www.lowdenhillswinery.com
Hours: Mar.–Oct., Sat.–Mon. 11 a.m.–
4 p.m., rest of the year Sat. only

MANNINA CELLARS
1370 Shade Tree Lane, Walla Walla
(509) 529 5760
www.manninacellars.com
Hours: Not open to the public

MORRISON LANE WINERY
201 West Main Street, Walla Walla
(509) 526 0229
www.morrisonlane.com
Hours: Fri.–Mon. noon–6 p.m.
or by appointment

NICHOLAS COLE CELLARS
705 Berney Drive, Walla Walla
(509) 525 0608
www.nicholascolecellars.com
Hours: By appointment

NORTHSTAR
1736 JB George Road, Walla Walla
1 (866) 486 7828
www.northstarmerlot.com
Hours: Wed.–Sat. 10 a.m.–4 p.m., Sun.
11 a.m.–4 p.m. or by appointment

PATIT CREEK CELLARS
507 E Main, Dayton
(509) 382 4860
www.patitcreekcellars.com
Hours: Sat. 11 a.m.–5 p.m. during
summer. Call for other hours.

PATIT CREEK CELLARS
TASTING ROOM
4 South Fourth Street, Walla Walla
(509) 382 1357
www.patitcreekcellars.com
Hours: Apr. 1 –Dec. 31, Fri. and Sat.
Call for hours.

PATRICK M. PAUL VINEYARDS
107 South 3rd Avenue, Walla Walla
(509) 526 0676
Hours: May–Nov., Sun.–Thu. 1 p.m.–
5 p.m., Sat. 11 a.m.–5 p.m., rest of year
Mon.–Sat. 11 a.m.–5 p.m., Sun. 1 p.m.–
5 p.m. Closed Wed. between Dec.
and Apr.

PEPPER BRIDGE WINERY
1704 JB George Road, Walla Walla
(509) 525 6502
www.pepperbridge.com
Hours: Daily 10 a.m.–4 p.m.

RED DIAMOND WINERY
Paterson
www.reddiamondwine.com
Hours: Not open to the public

REININGER WINERY
5858 W Highway 12, Walla Walla
(509) 522 1994
www.reiningerwinery.com
Hours: Daily 10 a.m.–6 p.m. (closes at
5 p.m. during winter)

RULO WINERY
3525 Pranger Road, Walla Walla
(509) 525 7856
www.rulowinery.com
Hours: By appointment

RUSSELL CREEK WINERY
301 Aeronca Avenue, Walla Walla
Regional Airport
(509) 386 4401
www.russellcreek-winery.com
Hours: Daily 11 a.m.–4 p.m.

SAPPHIRE MOUNTAIN CELLARS
883 Biscut Ridge Road, Dixie
(509) 522 0961
www.sapphiremountaincellars.com
Hours: By appointment, call for
directions

SAPOLIL CELLARS TASTING ROOM
425 "B" Street, Walla Walla
(509) 520 5258
www.sapolilcellars.com
Hours: Call for details

SAVIAH CELLARS
1979 JB George Road, Walla Walla
(509) 520 5166
www.saviahcellars.com
Hours: Apr.-Nov., Sat. 11 a.m.–5 p.m.
or by appointment

SEVEN HILLS WINERY
212 North Third Avenue, Walla Walla
(509) 529 7198
www.sevenhillswinery.com
Hours: May-Oct., Thu.-Sat.
11 a.m.–4 p.m.

SKYLITE CELLARS
7 North 2nd Avenue, Walla Walla
(509) 529 8000
www.skylitecellars.com
Hours: Call for details

SPRING VALLEY VINEYARD
1663 Corkrum Road, Walla Walla
(509) 521 1506
www.springvalleyvineyard.com
Hours: By appointment

SPRING VALLEY VINEYARD
TASTING ROOM
7 South 4th Street, Walla Walla
(509) 525 1506
www.springvalleyvineyard.com
Hours: Fri. and Sat. 11 a.m.–4 p.m.

STEPHENSON CELLARS
755 B Street, Walla Walla
Regional Airport
(509) 301 9004
www.stephensoncellars.com
Hours: Sat. 1 p.m.–4 p.m.
or by appointment

SYZYGY
405 East Boeing Avenue, Walla Walla
Regional Airport
(509) 522 0484
www.syzygywines.com
Hours: Mar.-Dec., Sat. 11 a.m.–4 p.m.

TAMARACK CELLARS
700 "C" Street, Walla Walla
Regional Airport
(509) 526 3533
www.tamarackcellars.com
Hours: Mar.-Dec., Sat. 10 a.m.–4 p.m.
or by appointment

THREE RIVERS WINERY
5641 West Highway 12, Walla Walla
(509) 526 9463
www.threeriverswinery.com
Hours: Daily 10 a.m.–6 p.m. Closed
Christmas, Thanksgiving and New
Year's Day.

VA PIANO VINEYARDS
1793 JB George Road, Walla Walla
(509) 529 0900
www.vapianovineyards.com
Hours: By appointment

WALLA WALLA VILLAGE WINERY
107 South 3rd Avenue, Walla Walla
(509) 525 9463
www.wallawallavillagewinery.com
Hours: Open daily 11 a.m.–5 p.m.,
closed Wed.

WALLA WALLA VINTNERS
225 Vineyard Lane, Walla Walla
(509) 525 4724
www.wallawallavintners.com
Hours: Sat. 10:30 a.m.–4:30 p.m.

WATERBROOK WINERY
31 E Main Street, Walla Walla
(509) 522 1262
www.waterbrook.com
Hours: Daily 10:30 a.m.–4:30 p.m.

WATERS WINERY
416 North 2nd Avenue, Walla Walla
(509) 525 1590
www.waterswinery.com
Hours: Call for hours

WHITMAN CELLARS
1015 W Pine Street, Walla Walla
(509) 529 1142
www.whitmancellars.com
Hours: Daily 11 a.m.–5 p.m.

WOODWARD CANYON WINERY
11920 W Highway 12, Lowden
(509) 525 4129
www.woodwardcanyon.com
Hours: Daily 10 a.m.–5 p.m.

YELLOW HAWK CELLAR
395 Yellowhawk Street, Walla Walla
(509) 529 1714
www.yellowhawkcellar.com
Hours: By appointment

# Wineries of the Spokane Area

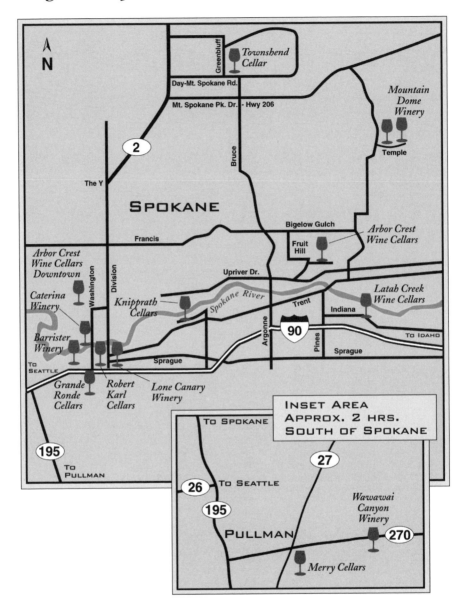

## Wineries of the Spokane Area

ARBOR CREST WINE CELLARS
4705 North Fruithill Road, Spokane
(509) 927 9463
www.arborcrest.com
Hours: Open daily noon–5 p.m.

BARRISTER WINERY
1213 W Railroad Avenue, Spokane
(509) 465 3591
www.barristerwinery.com
Hours: Open Sat. 10 a.m.–4 p.m. and
1st Fri. of each month 5 p.m.–8 p.m.

CATERINA WINERY
905 North Washington Street
Spokane
(509) 328 5069
www.caterinawinery.com
Hours: Noon–5 p.m. daily, wine bar
5 p.m.–midnight Fri. and Sat.

GRANDE RONDE CELLARS
Freeman Center, 906 W Second
Spokane
(509) 455 8161
www.granderondecellars.com
Hours: Wed.–Sat. noon–6 p.m.

KNIPPRATH CELLARS
5634 East Commerce Avenue
Spokane
(509) 534 5121
www.knipprath-cellars.com
Hours: Thu.–Sun. noon–5 p.m.
or by appointment

LATAH CREEK WINE CELLARS
13030 E Indiana Avenue, Spokane
(509) 926 0164
www.latahcreek.com
Hours: Daily 9 a.m.–5 p.m.

LONE CANARY WINERY
109 South Scott Street, B2, Spokane
(509) 534 9062
www.lonecanary.com
Hours: Thu.–Sun. noon–5 p.m.
or by appointment

MERRY CELLARS
245 SE Paradise Street, Pullman
(509) 338 4699
www.merrycellars.com
Hours: Fri. 4 p.m.–8 p.m., Sat.
noon–8 p.m.

MOUNTAIN DOME WINERY
16315 E Temple Road, Spokane
(509) 928 2788
www.mountaindome.com
Hours: Sat. 11 a.m.–5 p.m. during
summer, or by appointment

NODLAND CELLARS
11616 E Mongomery Dr, Ste 69
Spokane Valley
(509) 927 7770
www.nodlandcellars.com
Hours: Call for details

ROBERT KARL CELLARS
115 W Pacific Avenue, Spokane
(509) 363 1353
www.robertkarl.com
Hours: Sat. noon–5 p.m.
or by appointment

TOWNSHEND CELLAR
16112 North Greenbluff Road, Colbert
(509) 238 1400
www.townshendcellar.com
Hours: Fri.–Sun. noon–6 p.m.
or by appointment

WAWAWAI CANYON WINERY
5602 State Route 270, Pullman
(509) 338 4916
www.wawawaicanyon.com
Hours: Please call to confirm hours

# Wineries of North Central Washington

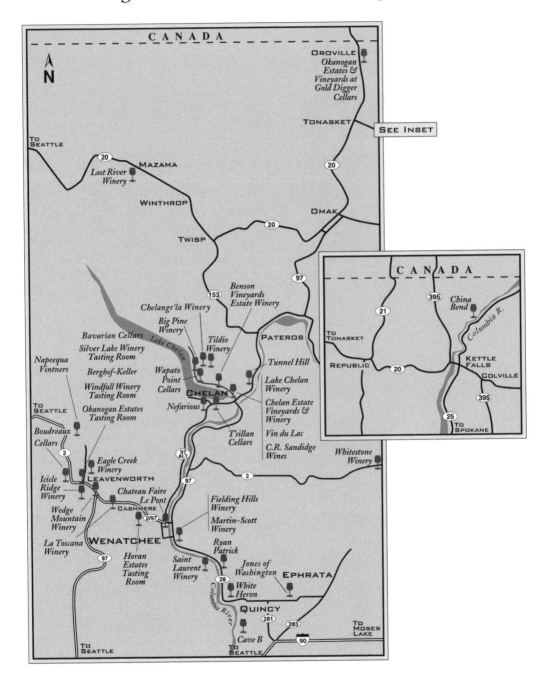

# Wineries of North Central Washington

BAVARIAN CELLARS
208 9th Street (B), Leavenworth
(509) 548 7717
Hours: Mon.,Thu. and Fri. noon-
5:30 p.m., Sat. noon-6 p.m., Sun.
noon-5 p.m. Call to confirm.

BERGHOF KELLER WINERY
11695 Duncan Road, Leavenworth
(509) 548 5605
www.berghofkeller.com
Hours: Open Daily 1 p.m.-5 p.m.

BIG PINE WINERY
280 Summit Boulevard, Manson
(509) 687 0889
www.bigpinewinery.com
Hours: Daily noon-7 p.m.

BOUDREAUX CELLARS
4551 Icicle Creek Road, Leavenworth
(509) 548 5858
www.boudreauxcellars.com
Hours: By appointment

C.R. SANDIDGE WINES
137 East Woodin Ave, Chelan
(509) 682 3704
www.crsandidgewines.com
Hours: Seasonal, call ahead

CAVE B ESTATE WINERY
348 Silica Road NW, Quincy
(509) 785 3500
www.caveb.com
Hours: Summer; Sun.-Thu. 11 a.m.-
5:30 p.m., Fri.-Sat. 11 a.m.-7 p.m.
Call for winter hours.

CHATEAU FAIRE LE PONT
1 Vineyard Way, Wenatchee
(509) 667 9463
www.fairelepont.com
Hours: Open Sat.-Thu. 11 a.m.-6 p.m.
and Fri. until 8 p.m.

CHELAN ESTATE VINEYARDS
& WINERY
755 S Lakeshore Road, Chelan
(509) 682 5454
Hours: Open weekends and some
weekdays; call for hours

CHELANGR'LA WINERY
3310 Manson Blvd, Manson
(509) 687 9746
www.chelangrla.com
Hours: Apr. 1-Nov. 1 daily,
noon-6 p.m. then weekends and
special events only

CHINA BEND VINEYARD & WINERY
3751 Vineyard Way, Kettle Falls
1 (800) 700 6123
www.chinabend.com
Hours: April-Oct., noon-5 p.m.
Off season by appointment

EAGLE CREEK WINERY
10037 Eagle Creek Road, Leavenworth
(509) 548 7668
www.eaglecreekwinery.com
Hours: May-Oct., daily 11 a.m.-4 p.m.
or by appointment

FIELDING HILLS WINERY
1401 Fielding Hills Drive
East Wenatchee
(509) 884 2221
www.fieldinghills.com
Hours: By appointment

GAMACHE VINTNERS
23509 North Dallas Road, Richland
(509) 628 8156
www.gamachevintners.com
Hours: By appointment

HORAN ESTATES WINERY
(TASTING ROOM)
600 Apple Annie Avenue, Cashmere
(509) 662 7573
www.horanestateswinery.com
Hours: Call for details

ICICLE RIDGE WINERY
8977 North Road, Peshastin
(509) 548 7851
www.icicleridgewinery.com
Hours: Daily noon-5 p.m.
or by appointment

JONES OF WASHINGTON
903 A Street SE, Quincy
(509) 787 3537
www.jonesofwashington.com
Hours: Call for details

LA TOSCANA WINERY
9020 Foster Road, Cashmere
(509) 548 5448
www.latoscanawinery.com
Hours: By appointment

LAKE CHELAN WINERY
3519 State Road 150, Chelan
(509) 687 9463
www.lakechelanwinery.com
Hours: Daily 11 a.m.-6 p.m.

LOST RIVER WINERY
26 Highway 20, Winthrop
(509) 996 2888
www.lostriverwinery.com
Hours: Fri.-Sat. 11 a.m.-5 p.m.

MARTIN-SCOTT WINERY
3400 10th Street SE, East Wenatchee
(509) 886 4596
www.martinscottwinery.com
Hours: Sat. noon-5 p.m.
or by appointment

NAPEEQUA VINTNERS
18820 Beaver Valley Road, Plain
(206) 930 7501
www.napeequa.com
Hours: Open holiday weekends
and by appointment

NEFARIOUS CELLARS
495 S Lakeshore Road, Chelan
(509) 682 9505
www.nefariouscellars.com
Hours: Thu.-Mon. 11 a.m.-6 p.m.
or Tue. and Wed. by chance

OKANAGAN ESTATE
TASTING ROOM
285 Highway 2, Leavenworth
(509) 548 9883
www.okanoganwine.com
Hours: Daily 10:30a.m.-6 p.m.
(check hours in the off season)

OKANAGAN ESTATES AND GOLD
DIGGER CELLARS
1205 Main Street (Highway 97)
Oroville
(509) 476 2736
www.golddiggercellars.com
Hours: Daily 11 a.m.–5 p.m.

RYAN PATRICK VINEYARDS
80 4th Street, Rock Island
(509) 667 9861
www.ryanpatrickvineyards.com
Hours: By appointment

SAINT LAURENT WINERY
4147 Hamlin Road, Malaga
(509) 888 9463
www.saintlaurent.net
Hours: Mon.–Sun. noon–5 p.m.

SILVER LAKE WINERY
(TASTING ROOM)
715 Front Street, Leavenworth
(509) 548 5788
www.silverlakewinery.com
Hours: Daily 11 a.m.–6 p.m.

SMALLWOOD'S HARVEST
Peshastin
(509) 548 4196
www.smallwoodsharvest.com
Hours: Visitors welcome, call for
hours and directions

TILDIO WINERY
70 East Wapato Lake Road, Manson
(509) 687 8463
www.tildio.com
Hours: Summer, daily noon–6 p.m.;
winter, weekends only noon–5 p.m.

TSILLAN CELLARS, VINEYARDS
& WINERY
3875 Highway 97A, Chelan
(509) 682 9463
www.tsillancellars.com
Hours: Open daily; summer, 11 a.m.–
7 p.m., winter, 11 a.m.–5 p.m.

TUNNEL HILL
37 Highway 97A, Chelan
(509) 682 5695
www.tunnelhillwinery.com
Hours: Open weekends during the
summer and by appointment

VIN DU LAC
105 Highway 150, Chelan
(866) 455 9463
www.vindulac.com
Hours: Open daily 11 a.m.–6 p.m.
(May–Sep. open till 7 p.m.)

WAPATO POINT CELLARS
200 Quetilquasoon Road, Manson
(509) 687 4000
www.wapatopointcellars.com
Hours: Daily 11 a.m.–7 p.m.

WEDGE MOUNTAIN WINERY
9534 Saunders Road, Peshastin
(509) 548 7068
www.wedgemountainwinery.com
Hours: Thu.–Mon. 10 a.m.–6 p.m.
(closes at 5 p.m. in winter)

WESTCOTT BAY ORCHARDS
COUNTRY-STYLE CIDER
43 Anderson Lane, Friday Harbor
(360) 378 3880
Hours: Call for details (not open to the
public at time of printing)

## Wineries of Southwest Washington and the Columbia Gorge Area

BETHANY VINEYARD AND WINERY
4115 NE 259th Street, Ridgefield
(360) 887 3525
www.bethanyvineyards.com
Hours: Sat. 11 a.m.–6 p.m.
or by appointment

CAPSTONE CELLARS
4305 Pacific Way, Longview
(360) 577 3525
www.capstonecellars.com
Hours: Call for details

CASCADE CLIFFS VINEYARD
& WINERY
8866 Highway 14, Wishram
(509) 767 1100
www.cascadecliffs.com
Hours: Daily 10 a.m.–6 p.m.

COLUMBIA GORGE WINERY
& KLICKITAT CANYON WINES
6 Lyle-Snowden Road, Lyle
(509) 365 2900
www.columbiagorgewinery.com
Hours: By appointment only

COR CELLARS
151 Old Highway 8, Lyle
(509) 365 2744
www.corcellars.com
Hours: Between Memorial Day and
Labor Day, Fri.–Sun. 11 a.m.–5 p.m.

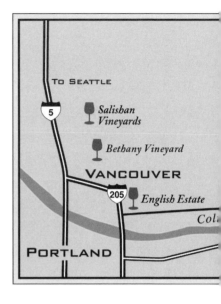

ENGLISH ESTATE
17908 SE 1st Street, Vancouver
(360) 772 5141
www.englishestatewinery.com
Hours: Thu.–Sun. noon–6 p.m. or by
appointment

MAJOR CREEK CELLARS
White Salmon
www.majorcreekcellars.com
Hours: Not open to the public at time
of print

MARSHAL'S WINERY & VINEYARD
150 Oak Creek Road, Dallesport
(509) 767 4633
www.marshalswinery.com
Hours: Daily 9 a.m.–7 p.m.

MARYHILL WINERY
9774 Highway 14, Goldendale
1 (877) 627 9445
www.maryhillwinery.com
Hours: Daily 10 a.m.–6 p.m.

SALISHAN VINEYARDS
35011 North Fork Ave., LaCenter
(360) 263 2713
www.washingtonwine.org
Hours: May–Dec., Sat. 1 p.m.–5 p.m.
or by appointment

# Wineries of the Southwest Washington and the Columbia Gorge Area

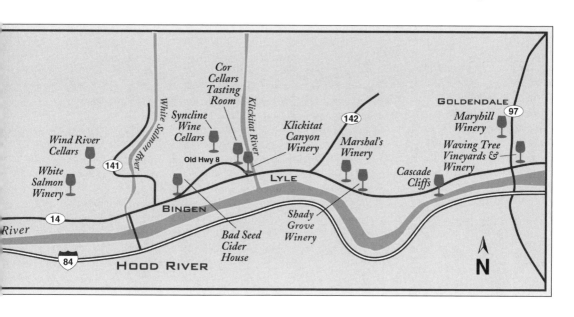

SHADY GROVE WINERY
Mile Marker 82.3, Highway 14
Dallesport
(509) 767 1400
www.shadygrovewinery.com
Hours: Fri.–Sun. 11 a.m.–6 p.m.

SYNCLINE WINE CELLARS
111 Balch Road, Lyle
(509) 365 4361
www.synclinewine.com
Hours: Jun.–Sep., Fri.–Sun.
noon–6 p.m.

WAVING TREE VINEYARD & WINERY
2 Maryhill Highway, Goldendale
(509) 773 6552
www.wavingtreewinery.com
Hours: Memorial Day–Labor Day
open daily ; Apr.–May and Sep.–Nov.,
Fri.–Sun., hours always 9 a.m.–5 p.m.

WHITE HERON CELLARS
10035 Stuhlmiller Road, Quincy
(509) 797 9463
www.whiteheronwine.com
Hours: Thu.–Mon. 11 a.m.–6 p.m.

WHITE SALMON VINEYARD
Underwood
(509) 493 4640
www.whitesalmonvineyard.com
Hours: By appointment

WHITESTONE WINERY
115 NE Main Street, Wilbur
(509) 647 5325
www.whitestonewinery.com
Hours: Call or check website for
current hours

WINDFALL WINERY
(TASTING ROOM)
843 Front Street, Leavenworth
(509) 548 7348
www.windfallwine.com
Hours: Daily 11 a.m.–5 p.m.

WIND RIVER CELLARS
196 Spring Creek Road, Husum
(509) 493 2324
www.windrivercellars.com
Hours: Daily 10 a.m.–6 p.m., Closed
Dec. 15–Jan. 1.

XS VINTNERS
PO Box 12591, Everett
(425) 210 1554
www.xsvwines.com
Hours: Call for details

# Index

## Special Thanks

A special thanks to everyone who went out of their way
to help us put this book together. It would not have been
possible without your time, advice and generosity. Of special
note are Michael Strang, Angela McLean, Elaine Jones and
Gavin Forbes. Thank you to our parents for their inspiration,
enthusiasm and encouragement. Thanks also to Brent and
Sarah for letting us raid their garden. And Blair, we will
always miss you.

## Further Reading

For further reading on the food and wine of the Pacific
Northwest two excellent magazines are *Wine Press Northwest*
and *Northwest Palate*.

## About the Authors

**Troy Townsin** was born in Melbourne, Australia, and worked as an actor and playwright before embarking on a round-the-world backpacking extravaganza. After establishing a career in hospitality he returned to Melbourne and earned a Bachelor of Arts in International Studies, taking semesters in Malaysia, Turkey and the UK. While studying in Malaysia he met his wife, Cheryl-Lynn. After graduating, he worked for the United Nations Information Centre in London before taking a job as an event reporter. In 2003, he won the prestigious Travel Writer of the Year award with *TNT Magazine UK*. After moving to the Pacific Northwest in 2004, Troy co-authored *Cooking with BC Wine*, a 2005 Gourmand World Cookbook Award winner. In 2006 Troy ran a weekly "Time for Wine" column on CBC radio.

**Cheryl-Lynn Townsin** was born and raised in British Columbia. She completed her Bachelor of Commerce in International Business at the University of Victoria. Pursuing an international career in business she has worked and traveled extensively throughout South East Asia, Europe and the Middle East. Eventually the lure of the Pacific Northwest proved too much and she returned to be married in 2004. Cheryl-Lynn co-authored *Cooking with BC Wine* and is currently coordinating international programs for Royal Roads University.